Pineapple Town | **HAWAII**

Edward Norbeck

Pineapple Town | **HAWAII**

University of California Press
Berkeley and Los Angeles
1959

University of California Press
Berkeley and Los Angeles, California
Cambridge University Press
London, England
Library of Congress Catalog Card Number: 59-5745
© 1959 by the Regents of the University of California
Printed in the United States of America
Designed by Ward Ritchie

PUBLISHED WITH THE ASSISTANCE OF A
GRANT FROM THE FORD FOUNDATION

To My Wife

Preface

This book is an account of a Hawaiian pineapple plantation and the community in which its employees live. Its aims are not solely descriptive. The company town represents a class of communities with distinctive characteristics. An attempt is made to outline these traits as they are revealed in the pineapple plantation community of Maunaloa, Molokai, and to point out factors which have brought them into existence. The influence of techniques of pineapple husbandry and the demands of industrial employment upon the lives of employees and their families are explored analytically with special emphasis on the changes which time has brought.

Observations are made also on the characteristics of Hawaiian pineapple plantation communities as a group. I am well aware that no single pineapple town of Hawaii is truly typical of all. Each is distinctive, but all have much in common. All are "owned" and operated by business corporations, a condition which profoundly affects community life and social relationships. All have been shaped in varying detail but common outline by circumstances peculiar to Hawaii. All have common problems and have been similarly affected by changing socioeconomic conditions of Hawaii and the rest of the world. What is true of Maunaloa is in large measure true of all other Hawaiian pineapple towns.

The data assembled here were derived in part from five years of service, from 1938 to 1943, as an administrative employee of Libby, McNeill and Libby, the corporation which operates Maunaloa plantation. During most of this period I lived in Maunaloa or one of two other plantation towns of the corporation on the islands of Oahu and Maui. In the course of my work I visited Maunaloa often, and I resided there continuously for fifteen months during 1940 and 1941. Military service took me away from Hawaii in 1943, and I did not see Maunaloa again until late 1946, when a visit of a few weeks gave me some idea of post-

war conditions. After an absence of ten years, I next returned to Maunaloa in 1956, during the summer vacation from my teaching duties as an anthropologist at the University of California at Berkeley. Many of the data I have used were gathered by my wife and myself at this time.

Some knowledge of plantation communities other than those in which I have resided was gained during the period from 1938 to 1942 by brief visits, often social in nature, to most of the other Hawaiian pineapple towns. In 1956 officials of several plantations were interviewed regarding the industry in general, and factual information on personnel and mechanization was gathered for comparative purposes on four plantations in addition to Maunaloa.

Writers of books such as this customarily veil the identity of the community as a means of protecting both the people described and themselves. I have not attempted to do so because no Hawaiian pineapple plantation community can be made truly anonymous. Even a slight knowledge of the Hawaiian Islands makes identification easy. So far as possible, however, the identity of persons mentioned in these pages is concealed. Certainly I shall make no ethical judgments concerning them. The moral attributes of the people described are of concern to the objectives of this study only as they affect relations among the people themselves. Such ethical judgments as appear here are included because they are thought to shed light on attitudes and interpersonal relations. All represent the sentiments of the people themselves and are so identified. For statements that may appear unflattering, I am truly concerned and wish to assure the reader that no censure or condemnation is intended on my part. For errors in fact I offer sincere apologies.

I owe hearty thanks to the management of Libby, McNeill and Libby for permission to pursue this study in 1956, for allowing my family and myself to reside in the plantation community, and for providing other useful aid. The privilege of access to records maintained by the plantation on personnel and other matters was particularly helpful, yielding a rapid and rich harvest of vital information which would otherwise have required many weeks of effort to collect. I am warmly grateful to the employees of the plantation and other residents of the community, many of whom were old friends at the time of our residence in 1956, for companionship as well as for patience in answering our many questions. Special thanks are due Mr. and Mrs. Harry W. Larson and Mrs. Sally Sunn for many things. I am indebted to the Committee on Research of the University of California at Berkeley for financial support.

Contents

Illustrations

Maps

| *Tables*

I | *Introduction*

Little about the Hawaiian pineapple plantation may be called truly indigenous. The crop is an alien from South America; most of the employees are recent migrants from other lands or the offspring of unions between immigrants and native Polynesians; and operation of the plantations follows precedents long established in other parts of the world. Even the soil, treated for years with foreign nutrients and other chemicals, may hardly be described as aboriginal. But nativeness in human culture is everywhere relative, a composite derived from many sources and molded into distinctive form. The Hawaiian pineapple plantation and the community associated with it are surely indigenous in the sense that their duplicates may not be found elsewhere. They have a unique flavor arising from the local conditions under which they emerged and grew.

The pineapple industry of Hawaii has had only a brief history, but today it represents a level of scientific and commercial development of horticulture seldom reached elsewhere. Pineapples were introduced to Hawaii early in the nineteenth century, but commercial cultivation and canning did not begin until much later, just after the turn of the twentieth century. Growth of the industry under the impetus of an expanding world market was rapid, and pineapple production had become large-scale by the third decade of the century. By this time the success of pineapple as an industrial crop had attracted the attention of mainland fruit-packing corporations, which established plantations in Hawaii during that decade.

Second only to sugar in importance in the economy of the Islands, the annual Hawaiian production of pineapples comprises about three-fourths of the world total. The annual gross revenue exceeds $100,000,-000, derived from the cultivation of approximately 73,000 acres. The industry provides year-round employment for about 6,000 regular employees and 4,000 intermittent employees. During the summer months, an additional 10,000 or more persons are engaged. Thus the peak employment is approximately 20,000 workers.

Pineapples are raised on fourteen plantations on the islands of Oahu, Maui, Kauai, Molokai, and Lanai, and canned on the islands of Oahu, Maui, and Kauai, each of which has three canneries. Fruit raised on Molokai and Lanai is shipped by barges to Honolulu for canning. Plantations are owned and operated by nine corporations, two of which are mainland concerns and account for over 40 per cent of the total annual production. All corporations, Hawaiian and mainland, jointly support an extensive program of coöperative agricultural research carried out by the Pineapple Research Institute, which is staffed by highly trained specialists. Reported to have an annual operating budget of about $1,000,000, it is one of the largest, privately financed agronomical research institutes in the world.

At the beginning of the twentieth century the incipient industry was faced with the problem of developing techniques of husbandry to allow extensive and profitable cultivation. This problem was quickly met under the economic conditions of the time. Profitable techniques of pineapple culture were developed early, and the market continued to expand. The subsequent history of plantation husbandry has seen much change and development, with both the Pineapple Research Institute and the independent research of plantation companies contributing to the solution of problems as they arose. Improved technology has averted at least two imminent crises, the second of which led eventually to profound social changes in the plantation communities.

In the late 1920's the industry was threatened by a serious disease of pineapple plants called mealy bug wilt. The Pineapple Research Institute developed measures of control in time to avert catastrophe, and mealy bug wilt is no longer considered a serious problem.

A second threat emerged at the end of World War II. Faced with swollen production costs and heavily increased competition from foreign pineapple and mainland fruits, the industry found itself in a critical position. Hourly rates for laborers had mounted steadily, from 25 cents in 1939 to a minimum of $1.24 for adult males in 1956. Virtually all raw materials and machinery were imported, and the industry's own product had to be exported at high rates of ocean freight.

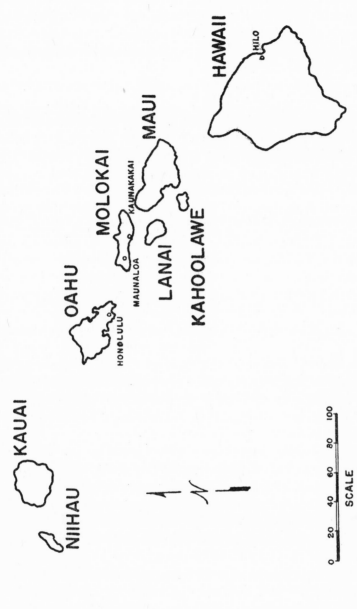

The Hawaiian Islands

Fringe benefits for employees had risen to a figure several times that prevailing before the war. Drastic economies were necessary to prevent pineapple from becoming outpriced by other fruits and the Hawaiian industry being relegated to a small-scale enterprise producing a high-priced luxury product.

It was clear that operations must be changed to increase production and cut costs, in particular to pare the costs of now expensive labor. The obvious answer lay in greater mechanization and higher crop yields. No ready-made solutions were available in the form of mechanical equipment suited to local needs, or techniques of husbandry developed elsewhere.

Under the spur of threatened financial failure, money-saving innovations arose from individual corporations and from the Research Institute and spread rapidly from plantation to plantation. In the decade following the end of World War II, techniques of plantation operation underwent extensive change. The plantations of today are remarkable examples of the welding of commercial enterprise and applied science.

Problems connected directly with the soil, insect pests, rainfall, and other purely horticultural considerations have always faced the industry, but they have sometimes been dwarfed in importance by the thornier problem of securing an adequate supply of labor. Long before the inception of the pineapple industry, native Hawaiians had been reduced by European diseases to a tiny fraction of their former numbers. The few available Hawaiians and part Hawaiians were temperamentally unsuited to plantation life or were so judged. Following the pattern long since established by Hawaiian corporations operating sugar plantations, the pineapple companies solved the problem by using foreign labor, principally the unrepatriated residue of earlier importations of men who had reached Hawaii under labor contracts with sugar companies. During the history of the pineapple industry, labor under contract has constituted only a small part of the total, but labor contracts have been important as the agency by which plantation and cannery employees originally reached Hawai.

Plantation labor in Hawaii has an interesting history of its own, but much of it does not concern the pineapple industry, which entered importantly into that history only in its later phases. The roster of nations and peoples from which Hawaiian sugar and pineapple plantation labor was drawn is large and impressive. In roughly chronological order of importation, the list includes Chinese, Portuguese, Japanese, Puerto Ricans, Koreans, and Filipinos.

Drawn from the economically pressed classes of their nations, the contract laborers were impoverished people who had little or no formal education. As foreign plantation laborers, their social status was low, a circumstance which was by no means new to them. Rather than return to an uncertain future in their native lands, many chose to remain in Hawaii when their contracts were fulfilled. They and their descendants form the bulk of the modern Hawaiian population. /

Many of the immigrants remained as plantation workmen until their retirement or death. Their descendants have entered plantation employment in relatively small numbers, usually as skilled workmen or supervisors. The most common pattern for the Hawaii-born is migration to the city of Honolulu or to towns, where they take employment as clerks, shopkeepers, and craftsmen, or become business and professional men.

To fill the gap created by the loss of imported laborers, plantations imported others until a sufficiently large reservoir of foreign labor had been created. Importation of labor ceased in 1931 and, despite slight shortages in the intervening "normal" years and irremediable shortages during World War II, was not resumed until 1946. In that year sugar and pineapple corporations jointly imported approximately 6,000 additional workmen from the Philippines. As of 1956 the labor supply was comfortably adequate, although the average age of plantation laborers was disturbingly high.

By the time the pineapple industry was well launched, only two groups of foreign workmen, the Japanese and the Filipinos, were of great numerical importance as plantation laborers. The majority of the unskilled labor force of the pineapple plantations of today is composed of Filipinos born and reared in the Philippine Islands who range in age from thirty-plus to sixty-five, the retirement age under the pension plans of all pineapple concerns. Few Hawaii-born Filipinos are included among regular plantation employees.

Employees of Japanese extraction, including a considerable number of Okinawans, comprise the second of the two principal groups. Because of the cultural differences between them, it is useful to distinguish two subdivisions among the Japanese, the Japan-born and the Hawaii-born. These distinctions are made by the Japanese themselves and have been adopted by other residents of Hawaii. The Japanese terms "issei" (literally, first generation; that is, first generation of Japanese in Hawaii) is used to signify persons born in Japan. "Nisei" (literally, second generation) means the first generation born in Hawaii. The term "sansei" (third generation) is used also, but the number of sansei adults among regular plantation employees is very small.

Issei are a vanishing part of the Hawaiian population. As of 1956, Japan-born Japanese in Hawaii totaled approximately 30,000, most of whom were old and many of whom had retired. The numerical strength of Japanese on the plantations comes through a combination of the vanishing issei, many of whom continue to work as laborers, and a fairly large number of nisei, who usually hold semiskilled, skilled, and supervisory positions.

All other categories of peoples conventionally distinguished among the modern Hawaiian population (except Negroes, who are few in number and confined chiefly to the city of Honolulu) are included in small numbers among plantation employees. With the exception of Puerto Ricans and some Cosmopolitans (persons of mixed descent), members of these groups are not often common laborers. Characteristically holding topmost plantation positions are a few Haoles—a word of Hawaiian derivation which today means persons of Caucasian race of any national background except Portuguese, who are consistently distinguished as Portuguese, or, unflatteringly, "Portugee." Also included is a sprinkling of Portuguese, Puerto Ricans, Cosmopolitans, and Chinese. Koreans and genetically pure Hawaiians are rare, and their total in Hawaii is also small.

Excluding seasonal employees, females are few and generally hold positions as secretaries or clerks. In former times a modest number of females, principally women from Okinawa, served as field laborers. A few of these aging women continue to work on some plantations today.

For about three months of the year, the number of employees is augmented by seasonal workers. Although pineapples mature or may be made to mature at any time of the year, they tend to be seasonal in fruiting. The period of heaviest harvesting and of the finest quality of fruit is June through August, when temporary employees must be hired. Depending upon the size of the crop, seasonal employees may total as much as 50 per cent of the regular force.

The composition of the seasonal crew is varied and different from that of the permanent personnel; except for those who are already members of the community—wives or children of regular employees— seasonal workers do not usually enter importantly into community life. Seasonal labor ordinarily includes a large number of boys and girls over sixteen years of age, most of whom are high-school students and sons and daughters of regular employees. Most of these adolescents and young adults have no desire to become regular employees, but are happy to have the opportunity of earning wages of $200 or more a month during the summer. Seasonal employees may include a small number of adult women, the wives of regular employees. Among both adolescents and adults of the seasonal force, the proportion with Cosmopolitan racial backgrounds tends to be greater than among regular employees.

In cultural background, country of birth, and racial affiliation, then, the employees of the modern Hawaiian pineapple plantations are a varied lot. Their immature children, many of whom are the offspring of interracial marriages, represent even greater variation.

Since inception in the nineteenth century of the policy of importing foreign labor to Hawaii, the practice of bringing in only adult males was often followed. Importation of wives and dependents was not encouraged for all racial-cultural groups and was left as the problem and expense of the individual employee. Most of the married Japanese laborers employed by the pineapple industry brought their wives and other dependents to Hawaii. Single men among them frequently imported picture brides from Japan or obtained brides from among the small number of single Japanese women in Hawaii who were dependents or widows of other immigrants. Issei rarely married women of another culture or race.

The less thrifty Filipinos, however, were frequently unable to accumulate enough money to pay for the passage of their wives and families. A large number continue to be absentee husbands, who may not have seen their wives and children for periods as long as forty years. Filipinos did not ordinarily marry picture brides. Some returned to the Philippines for the express purpose of finding brides, whom they brought back to Hawaii. But the ratio of males to females among the Filipinos of Hawaii remains today far out of balance in favor of males. Many Filipino men were unmarried young adults when they arrived in Hawaii, and for lack of eligible women in the new land, they are still single. Now well along in years, they are unlikely ever to wed. Other single Filipino men crossed racial and cultural lines to marry. The offspring of such unions have in the past several decades swelled the Cosmopolitan population of Hawaii, which in 1956 numbered more than 94,000 (of whom about 20,000 were part Filipino) and constituted approximately 19 per cent of the total population.

Plantation work in earlier times was done principally by hand, and required large numbers of laborers for successful operation. Unschooled, speaking little or no English, unacquainted with the culture of the land to which they had been transplanted, and bringing customs and values which were unacceptable in their new surroundings, the newly imported workmen needed protection, supervision, and guidance. At the time of their arrival they represented a cash investment for which a good return in labor was expected and necessary. Centralized communities not only provided otherwise unavailable housing and placed the new employees conveniently at hand but also ensured guidance and control over them.

Pineapple corporations followed a pattern earlier established by sugar corporations, a policy of paternalism for which many precedents existed in other parts of the world. Employees were housed in dwellings erected among or near the pineapple fields and were provided "free of charge" with living quarters, medical care, and other necessities. At the same time, managerial employees of the plantations exercised protective and sometimes heavy-handed paternalistic supervision over the workmen.

The plantation communities remain in Hawaii today, although they have changed much both in physical appearance and in the living conditions of their inhabitants. Characteristically, the corporation owns the dwellings and virtually all other buildings except those of the public school. It also provides facilities for worship and recreation. Shops, automobile service stations, and other business enterprises regarded as necessary for the community are commonly left to outsiders, who operate under the watchful eyes of plantation administrators. Communities are unincorporated, and community affairs are ordinarily handled by councils of employees and other residents, subject to the approval of company officials on issues which affect the corporation.

Pineapple corporations no longer provide their employees with perquisites—the rent-free housing, free nonindustrial medical care, and other services supplied in earlier days. Physicians and dentists in private practice maintain offices in the communities, or are otherwise within easy reach. Since the late 1940's, when all but one of the established Hawaiian pineapple plantations became almost wholly unionized, modest house rents have been charged and other formerly "free" services have become the expense of the individual.

Unless the conduct of employees interferes with the operations of the plantation, "the company" ordinarily does not directly intrude in their private affairs. Yet the shadow of the company is unavoidably everywhere, affecting the lives of all employees, from the topmost administrator to the lowliest laborer. This circumstance represents no plot, no deliberate intention, but is one of the inevitable characteristics of the plantation town, where the social relations and hierarchies of the working day are inescapably present at all times.

Conditions in company towns are unlike those of independent communities. The statement applies to the continental United States as well as to Hawaii. Company towns of Hawaii and their counterparts on the mainland share many characteristics, but those of the mainland are seldom so complex in racial or putatively racial considerations. Taking as a starting point the customary social hierarchy of any industrial concern—for that is what the plantation represents—and adding to it a set of racial-cultural hierarchies, we might reasonably expect the two to cut across each other in many ways and produce a complex social scheme. To the foregoing circumstances add rapidly changing technological and economic conditions of the United States as a whole and of the pineapple plantations in particular, and we might expect to find the conditions of plantation life dynamic rather than static. Those are in fact the conditions which exist and the events which have occurred. Some of these matters are peculiar to Hawaii, or even to individual plantations. Others are part and parcel of national conditions and trends of change. Still others are characteristic of the kind of community, whether it is located in Hawaii, California, Puerto Rico, or Brazil.

I shall discuss in detail one of these communities and the manner of life of its residents today. In the final chapters I shall describe the conditions of the past, and present such conclusions as seem warranted regarding the characteristics of the Hawaiian pineapple town and the nature of the changes that have taken place in it.

The community of Maunaloa lies isolated on the western end of the

Island of Molokai near the top of a rounded volcanic dome which rises sharply on its eastern face and slopes gradually to the sea on the west over a distance of several miles. On days when clouds do not obscure the view, the Island of Oahu, about thirty miles to the northwest, is clearly visible, and the lights of Honolulu may be seen at night.

The Island of Molokai, 260 square miles in area, is approximately thirty-eight miles long and varies from six to ten miles in width. A volcanic mountain reaching an altitude of 4,970 feet lies at its eastern extremity and forms the largest part of the island. At the western end of the island the volcanic dome of Mauna Loa (not to be confused with the well-known Mauna Loa of the Island of Hawai), from which the community of Maunaloa takes its name, rises at a sharp incline to a maximum eminence of 1,381 feet. Between the eastern mountain and the Mauna Loa dome is a saddle called the Hoolehua plain. The pineapple fields of Molokai are in the red lateritic soils of the lower and westerly slopes of the mountain, on the adjoining Hoolehua plain, and, continuing westward, on the slopes of Mauna Loa.

The population of Molokai totals approximately 5,000 persons, most of whom depend for livelihood directly or indirectly upon the three pineapple plantations on the island. Other industry is limited to the raising of a few thousand head of cattle and small-scale farming. Communities are few and small. Kaunakakai, with a population of approximately 1,100, is the largest town, the economic center, and the only port of the island. Maunaloa, second in size to Kaunakakai, is the only community in western Molokai. Approximately twelve miles from its nearest neighboring settlement, it lies seventeen miles from Kaunakakai.

Undeveloped for lack of water for irrigation, Molokai is known to the outside world chiefly because of its leper colony. On a small peninsula physically isolated from the main body of the island by a 2,000-foot cliff, the leper colony of Kalaupapa is also socially isolated. Off the beaten track for tourists, Molokai maintains the flavor of the Hawaii of yesteryear in greater degree than the more populous islands. The pineapple plantations of Molokai, however, are thoroughly modern.

Interisland travel is usually by airplane. There are several daily flights from the Honolulu airport to Molokai. It takes about thirty minutes to reach the airport in the center of the Hoolehua plain. Alight-

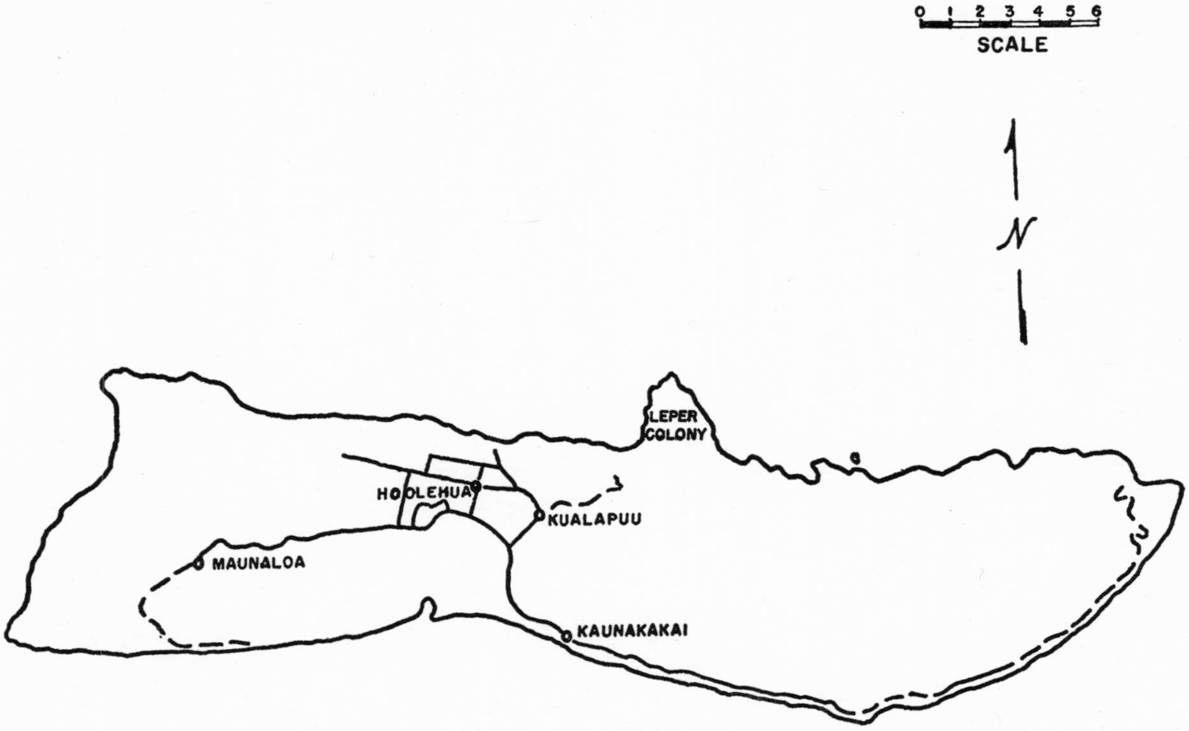

Island of Molokai

SCALE

0 1 2 3 4 5 6

N

LEPER COLONY

KUALAPUU

KAUNAKAKAI

HOOLEHUA

MAUNALOA

ing from the airplane, the visitor receives an immediate introduction to one of the characteristics of western Molokai—the fine dust of a burnt sienna color which is customarily called red. Sometimes invisible in the air and sometimes in highly visible clouds, the dust is present most of the year, settling heavily on exposed surfaces and sifting into seemingly inaccessible nooks and corners of house or car.

From the airport one travels by private car or taxi about twelve miles on a well-paved two-lane road to reach the plantation village of Maunaloa. The road runs through neatly planted fields of growing pineapple. Gray-green when the plants are young and adequately watered by rainfall, the fields are a motley of green, yellow, and withered brown sabers if they contain old plants that have been subjected to spells of dry weather, strong winds, and the trampling of many feet during weeding and harvesting. Other conspicuous vegetation is limited to *kiawe* (algarroba), a species of thorny tree. Thriving with little rainfall, it grows in shallow rocky washes and other areas poorly suited to the cultivation of pineapples.

Behind the traveler lie the pineapple fields of two rival plantations and, towering above them, the eastern mountain. Arid on its lower slopes, the mountain presents a scene of increasingly lush, wild vegetation as the eye travels upward to the crown of clouds at its peak. By contrast, the vista which lies ahead on the road to Maunaloa is one of stark, uninviting aridity. On the clifflike eastern boundary of Mauna Loa, the red-brown and yellow of exposed soil, volcanic cinders, and grass apparently lifeless most of the year predominate in the landscape. Here and there at lower altitudes are clumps of dusty *kiawe* trees. Skirting the edge of the sharp rise, the road takes an easy incline in rocky land containing many shallow rifts and gullies which nurture only wild grasses, *kiawe,* and a few cattle. The yellow-brown vista is relieved here and there in sheltered places by clumps of wind-torn eucalyptus and other exotic trees planted years earlier under a forestation program. Along the shoulders of the road, grasses are a rich green if rain has fallen recently.

The excellent road quickly brings the traveler into the pineapple fields on the gentle and rolling northwest slopes of Mauna Loa, from which a great expanse of vividly blue ocean and the Island of Oahu or the mass of clouds which mask it are visible to the west. Pineapple fields stretch for miles in every direction, rectangle after rectangle of growing plants bordered by the narrow red bands of field roads, in neat but monotonous geometric regularity. The eye welcomes the relief provided by changes in elevation and the occasional shallow gullies and eroded cuts of an angry red color. At the lower margins of the fields, dry grasses, rocky outcrops, *kiawe* trees, sand dunes, and occasional volcanic cinder cones create a desolate expanse of several miles until they terminate at the edge of the sea.

Nearing his destination, the traveler catches sight of two sizable white houses on the slope above him. Surrounded by vagrantly green lawns and wind-bowed vegetation, they look neat and substantial. At a lower elevation are many smaller dwellings, visible at first only as a cluster of green-painted galvanized iron roofs amid eucalyptus trees and Norfolk Island pines. The traveler passes the station where pineapples are loaded onto trucks for hauling to the port of Kaunakakai for shipment to the cannery in Honolulu, the mixing plant for insecticides and fertilizers, the service stations, and the shops for repair and maintenance of mechanical equipment. The journey terminates in the unnamed main street of Maunaloa. About one city block in length, it presents an uninspiring view of a few frame buildings, wind-battered trees, and a long expanse of closely trimmed and almost blossomless hibiscus hedges. The paved road comes to an end in the natural red soil of a field road leading into the pineapple fields.

From the main street, unpaved and unnamed roads branch to the left and right, narrow thoroughfares of raw, red soil which become seas of mud at the first heavy rain. Along these roads are the homes of the plantation workmen, small, closely spaced houses of light frame construction, stained, painted, or shingled, and usually streaked with accumulations of red dust. Tall Norfolk Island pines, of a surprisingly lush green, dwarf the cramped houses and narrow roads, which are made to appear still narrower by the row of black oil barrels placed at their edges to serve as trash and garbage containers.

Maunaloa is an ugly town. Many residents, recalling their first impression, describe it as appallingly ugly. The lack of beauty is in part due to the uniform dwellings erected without regard for aesthetic considerations, and crowded closely together. These words imply no censure of the corporation which built them, two or more decades ago. Similar dwellings may be found in any plantation community. At the time of their construction, they were superior to the houses which employees might individually erect or purchase, and were certainly far better than any houses they might have been able to rent outside the community.

Most of all, the ugliness of the community springs from circumstances beyond the control of its founders. Strong and frequent winds make it difficult to grow most varieties of trees and tender-leaved or tall vegetation. Even the hardy eucalpti which are planted as windbreaks have bowed and leafless tops.

More important than the wind in discouraging beauty are the ever-present red dust and the lack of adequate water to encourage the growth of ornamental vegetation. Annual rainfall at Maunaloa has averaged twenty-eight inches during the past thirty years, but there is considerable variation from year to year. These statistics suggest moisture adequate to allow the growth of fairly abundant vegetation, but they are deceptive. Most of the rain falls during a short period of the winter months. In certain years a few days of torrential rains have produced a statistically normal year of precipitation but an actual year of drought. Much of the rainfall, coming as it does in heavy downpours, runs off rapidly to the sea. These heavy and rapid runoffs carry with them large quantities of soil from the pineapple fields, and have greatly eroded the slopes of western Molokai. Several cuts in the fields, up to fifty feet in depth, mark the principal channels of drainage. As a result of this rapid erosion, the ocean, for distances of a mile or more from the shore of western Molokai, has an opaque red-brown color from the fine soil which goes into suspension easily and never completely settles because of the action of the tides and waves.

The Mauna Loa tableland has no permanent streams, and no water is captured there. Water for domestic consumption and for use in insecticide and fertilizer emulsions for the pineapple fields is transported by pipeline from the rainy slopes of eastern Molokai. Irrigation of pineapple plants, a practice recently adopted on a limited scale by other Hawaiian plantations cultivating fields with inadequate rainfall, has never been introduced for lack of water. Although the water resources of eastern Molokai are fairly abundant, little has yet been captured because of the great expense involved. The amount which reaches Maunaloa is small. It is frequently necessary to ration water during the summer by sharply curtailing or prohibiting the watering of lawns and other vegetation and repeatedly cautioning the residents of the community to conserve water.

Water is an extremely important matter at Maunaloa and a subject of concern both in domestic life and in plantation operations, where it is vital for insecticide and fertilizer sprays. The water which reaches Maunaloa is the subject of many scatological jokes because of its amber color, caused by the presence of fine soil in suspension, and, so it is said, by pigments from organic matter through which the water runs before it is captured. Maunaloa water is the horror of the new housewife until she learns that it is perfectly potable and, with the aid of bluing and laundry bleaches, serves quite well to launder clothing.

The lack of water, the dust, the wind, and their isolation from other communities annoy many residents of Maunaloa, but no one complains about the temperature, which most persons find exactly to their liking, and preferable to that of most other Hawaiian communities. Lying at an attitude exceeding 1,000 feet, the village of Maunaloa is usually a few degrees cooler than Honolulu or coastal towns. The mean temperature is approximately 72°. Extreme temperatures reaching or exceeding 90° are uncommon and of brief duration. The months of January through March, when temperatures may drop below 60° at night, are sometimes chilly and a few people then use portable heaters. The wind which carries dust and inhibits the growth of garden plants serves in more acceptable fashion to make even the hottest days of August and September, which ordinarily have the highest temperatures, seem pleasant.

II | *The Plantation*

Radiating for several miles from the community are the pineapple fields which brought it into existence. Ranking third in size and annual yield among the Hawaiian pineapple plantations, Maunaloa comprises nearly 10,000 acres of which all except the 200 acres allotted to the village are under cultivation. About three-fourths of the total acreage lies on the slopes of Mauna Loa, surrounding the community. The remaining fourth is in the Hoolehua plain, separated from the principal fields by the several miles of steep, rocky, and relatively soil-less eastern face of Mauna Loa and its immediate approaches.

All lands are leased from private owners. The Maunaloa fields lie within the boundaries of a cattle ranch, and consist of arid treeless lands formerly considered suitable only for the grazing of cattle and sheep. Between the borders of the fields and the ocean are several miles of ranch grazing lands, poor in soil, rainfall, and vegetation.

Hoolehua lands consist of numerous small but adjoining homestead plots owned by persons of Hawaiian or part-Hawaiian descent. Since only contiguous homesteads are under lease, many private holdings may be operated as continuous large sections.

The fine volcanic soil of the fields is of high natural fertility and considerable depth, in some areas exceeding forty feet. For lack of adequate rainfall to support other native crops, only sweet potatoes were grown in aboriginal times in the present Maunaloa fields, in tiny plots here and there in climatically favored areas. Considered too arid for pineapples, plantation land was first cultivated against the advice of some authorities on pineapple husbandry.

Although cultivation has been successful, the shortage of moisture has always been a major problem. Farming the driest pineapple lands in Hawaii, Maunaloa plantation has experienced heavier losses in yield in years of drought than other plantations. Certain of its agricultural practices, directed toward conserving moisture in the soil, differ for this reason from the practices of most other plantations. Although no more than hints of rain may fall for months at a time, the fine soil fortunately retains well the moisture from the few penetrating rains. Frequent condensation of dew at night, often so heavy that moisture drips from the eaves of houses like rain, also does much to compensate for the lack of rain.

Cultivation of the Maunaloa lands began in 1923. The Hoolehua fields, added in 1927, were soon operated as a separate plantation because of the difficulty of maintaining communication between the two areas. By modern standards, mechanical equipment on Molokai in the 1920's was scarce. Mules for plowing and cultivation and horses as the chief means of transportation were standard equipment. The unsurfaced dirt road which then linked the Maunaloa and Hoolehua fields wound a steep route up Mauna Loa. Even a light rain rendered the sharp bends dangerous on downward passage and almost impossible for motored vehicles to negotiate in ascent. Heavy rains might close the road to mechanical transport for days at a time. Administration of the two units as a single plantation was resumed in 1946, after the construction of a smooth, hard-surfaced highway which reduced the journey between them to a matter of a few minutes, safe in any weather. Some distinction between the two areas remains in plantation practices. Employees who work at Hoolehua do not ordinarily live in the community of Maunaloa, but instead live in privately owned dwellings. Employees residing at Maunaloa ordinarily work only in the Maunaloa fields, which are closer at hand.

The modern plantation is geared to produce maximum yields with minimum expenditures for labor, equipment, and supplies. To reach this objective, plantation operations are as highly mechanized as known technological aids will permit, and fields are kept in constant use. Under present horticultural practices, no fields are allowed to remain fallow. In an attempt to avoid peaks of seasonality and thereby avoid extreme fluctuation in the number of employees, fields are planted intermittently throughout the year. Thus at any given time the plantation has fields of plants in many stages of growth.

Pineapples are propagated by vegetative reproduction. The single variety of pineapple ordinarily raised, a hybrid called Smooth Cayenne introduced from Jamaica in 1886, only rarely produces a few seeds.

Cultivation from seed is undesirable because it would require a much longer period of growth as well as entailing various problems in plant genetics. Planting material consists of lateral shoots, called suckers or slips, depending upon their size and position on the parent plant, and the age of the parent plant. These shoots are removed from mature plants; their tops are trimmed, and they are then placed atop the parent plants for "curing." After a period of at least ten days they are ready for planting.

When a field is to be replanted, the old plants are knocked down and cut into pieces by a disking machine, but are allowed to remain on the surface of the ground, where they form a blanket several inches thick. At the same time the field is given a subsurface cultivation, under present practices the only cultivation it receives during the whole life cycle of the plants soon to be placed in it. A single machine performs many of the operations of planting. After disking machines have leveled the field and cut up the old plants, bedding machines perform the multiple and simultaneous operations of cultivating, fumigating, and fertilizing the soil, and of pushing aside disked plants from the narrow rows where new plants are to be placed. These machines at the same time lay long strips of heavy, tarred mulch paper, two feet in width, which bears marks at one-foot intervals at the extreme margins on both sides to indicate the points at which plants are to be inserted.

After the fields have been prepared, plants are transported from the mother fields by truck and distributed in piles along the roads in the new fields. Planting is a hand operation. Workmen insert the plants into the marked points on the mulch paper with the aid of a simple iron-bladed planting knife. The movements of a skilled worker are extremely rapid and he may plant several thousand shoots in the course of an eight-hour working day. Once inserted an inch or two in the soft ground beneath the mulch paper, the shoot has been planted. No tamping or watering is necessary. Pineapple shoots are viable for remarkably long periods, and if moisture in the ground is insufficient to allow growth at the time of planting, they remain alive as long as six months without added rainfall.

Depending upon the size of the planted shoots, the amount of subsequent rainfall, and other climatic factors, a pineapple field produces its first crop fifteen to twenty months after planting. Additional crops are produced at intervals of about twelve months. In the vocabulary of pineapple culture, the first crop is called the plant crop, and subsequent crops are called ratoons—first ratoon, second ratoon, and so on. If pineapple plants are allowed to bear several times before destruction, the ratoon crops tend gradually to mature during the summer months regardless of the time of original planting.

Most Hawaiian plantations harvest only two crops before replanting. Maunaloa plantation customarily takes three or four crops from its plants before disking and replanting, a practice which is followed in part to conserve ground moisture. Fields covered with a heavy growth of plants retain moisture better than newly planted fields or fields with young and therefore less dense vegetation.

A pineapple plant receives much attention during its life. At intervals of a few weeks it is sprayed with various fertilizers, chemical growth stimulants, insecticides, and weed killers. Any undesirable plant growth that is not killed by the increasingly effective chemical sprays must be removed by gangs of workmen with hoes. The Maunaloa practice of allowing disked pineapple plants to remain on the surface as a ground cover has, curiously, added the pineapple plant itself to the list of undesirable plants which must be removed without chemical aid. Portions of the old plants, presumably dead after disking, frequently take root between the rows of deliberately planted shoots and compete with them for nourishment. If allowed to grow, they would make progress by foot between the rows for harvesting or weeding extremely difficult.

Techniques of forcing crops are well developed but are ordinarily not extensively used. It is customary, however, to practice forcing when fields do not blossom uniformly and hence would produce a crop maturing unevenly and requiring expensive multiple harvesting. After blossoming has well begun, the recalcitrant plants are "hormoned" by liquid spray to induce blossoming and subsequent maturation of fruit about six months later.

By the time a pineapple field is ready for harvesting, the shoots, which projected five to seven inches above the ground at the time of planting, have grown into bushy, yucca-like growths three or four feet in height. The top of each plant is crowned by a single fruit, generally four to five pounds in weight at Maunaloa for the plant crop and a pound or more heavier on plantations with greater rainfall. The fruit of ratoon crops decreases in size with each crop.

Fruit is not harvested until it is fully ripe. Once picked, the pineapple essentially ceases to manufacture sugar. The field-ripened pineapple is incomparably superior in flavor, appearance, texture, and sugar content to the immaturely picked fresh pineapple sold in markets of the continental United States. But ripe fruit spoils rapidly and must therefore reach the processing plants quickly. Speed and efficiency are essential. Transported by trucks in large boxes each containing about four tons, harvested fruit ordinarily reaches the port of Kaunakakai within a few hours after picking. At Kaunakakai it is loaded for transport to Honolulu onto barges of approximately 250 tons capacity pulled by tugboats. Fruit ordinarily reaches the cannery in Honolulu within twenty-four hours after picking.

Yields per acre of pineapple are surprisingly great and probably exceed those of any other fruit. Under optimum conditions, the harvest of a plant crop may reach as high as forty tons per acre. Enormous quantities of fruit thus reach all pineapple canneries within a short time during the summer months, and techniques of handling must be both fast and efficient. Control over the harvesting of fifteen square miles of intensively cultivated and high-yielding fields requires the best possible channels of communication between fields, plantation head-quarters, and processing plant.

Profitable operation of the plantation means intense mechanization of all tasks. Wherever possible, machines have replaced men. In the cultivation of its 10,000 acres, Maunaloa plantation uses approximately 250 large pieces of mechanical equipment: harvesters, tractors, disking machines, multi-operation "bedding" machines, wheeled lifting machines, cranes, conventional automobiles, and a fleet of trucks of many kinds including spray trucks, supply trucks, and vehicles used for hauling pineapples. Maintenance of mechanical equipment is performed by a corps of mechanics, whose work includes the construction of experimental models of new machines.

Tracing the life cycle of the pineapple and the associated mechanical procedures, we find that preparation of fields for planting—disking, cultivation, fumigating, fertilizing, laying mulch paper, and making field roads at regular intervals—is done by machines. Fertilizers, growth stimulants, and insecticides are applied by means of airplane and tank truck. Spraying by air is done by a single plane and pilot of an outside company under a year-round, full-time contract. More important than airplane spraying, which may be suspended for days when winds are strong, is the older but well-developed technique of spraying by tank truck. Spray trucks operate throughout the year. Built with a 65-foot spray boom which extends at right angles from the body of the truck, a truck is able to reach and treat half of the 128-foot width of each block of plants in one sweep down a field road. A return trip on the adjoining field road completes the treatment.

Harvesting is done chiefly by machine. Like the spray units, mechanical harvesters consist of trucks to which 65-foot booms are attached at right angles. Extending over the rows of plants from the field road, the harvesting boom contains a conveyor belt which transports the harvested pineapples through a chute into a removable box. This box, in turn, forms the body of a transport truck backed into position in front of the harvester and propelled by the harvester while the box is being filled. After the truck has been loaded, it is replaced by a second waiting truck and transports its load of four tons of fruit to one of the loading stations. The loaded box is there removed by a mechanical lift and replaced by an empty box. Loaded boxes are next placed on larger trucks carrying either two or four of the huge containers and transported to the wharf, where cranes lift them onto waiting barges.

Actual picking of fruit is still manual labor. This operation is performed by crews of thirteen men to each harvester. Walking behind the booms in the aisles between rows of plants, the men stoop to pick the fruit with a wrenching movement, and rise to place it on the conveyor belt.

"Old" harvesting machines—less than a decade old but now regarded as obsolete equipment soon to be retired—require the services of two men for mechanical operation. "New" machines, upon which heaviest reliance is placed, are operated by one man. The many activities of the single operator include adjusting the height of the boom above the plants to compensate for changes in elevation in the rolling lands, driving the unit at a suitable rate of speed as determined by the quantity of fruit and the capabilities of the men who pick and place the fruit on the conveyor belt, and adjusting the movable mouth of the chute so that boxes are filled uniformly. Harvesters are equipped with fluorescent lights on the booms and floodlights far overhead for use in night harvesting at the height of the season.

To achieve the ease and rapidity of communication vital for efficient operation of the plantation, several expedient devices are in use. A fleet of automobiles and light trucks is used for the transport of plantation supervisors. Field roads, although unsurfaced, are kept smooth and allow passage swift enough to warrant a speed limit of thirty-five miles per hour in the fields. Key personnel are in constant communication with each other and with headquarters in the plantation office by means of a radio intercommunication system which includes fourteen automobiles, the office, the maintenance and repair shop, and the wharf. Communication with corporation headquarters in Honolulu by teletype is frequent. Intraplantation communication after work hours is ordinarily through the public telephone system. A daily meeting of key personnel serves to inform supervisors of plans and problems for discussion and settlement. A feature of the daily meeting is the projection of slides bearing statistics compiled by the office force on costs and production for the previous day's operations.

The development of more efficient techniques and mechanical devices is strongly encouraged by the corporation, which offers cash awards to employees whose suggestions are found acceptable and economically profitable. Extensive horticultural experimentation is conducted, with detailed records maintained of yields of fruit and similar matters.

Although the majority of plantation employees are laborers, there is much less hand labor today than in the past. The principal manual operations are stripping the fields for planting material, inserting plants into mechanically prepared beds, and picking ripe fruit to place it on mechanical conveyors. No practical device has yet been invented for mechanical planting or completely mechanical harvesting. Modern chemicals may, as a matter of fact, render picking more difficult, even though the advantages of their use far outweigh the disadvantages. Fields treated with synthetic plant hormones tend to develop fruit with long peduncles which often become dry and tough when the fruit is mature so that considerable pressure must be exerted to wrench the fruit from the plant.

Weed removal, formerly one of the most expensive operations because it was performed by crews of workmen with hoes, has become a relatively minor expense; as a hand operation it is necessary only for the few species of weeds which are unaffected by modern chemical weed killers.

Hand labor remains important also in harvesting fields which do not mature uniformly so that the ripe crop at any given time is too small and sparsely distributed to warrant the use of mechanical harvesters. Picking is then done by gangs of men who transport the fruit in burlap sacks to trucks moving along with them in the roadways. Mechanical harvesting, however, accounts for about 85 per cent of the annual crop.

As is customary on Hawaiian pineapple plantations, Maunaloa maintains a training program for its personnel. Many of the duties performed by plantation employees are unique and almost all of them are peculiar to this industry; hence virtually every category of employee must have training and experience. Nearly all employees are formally or informally trained on the plantation or have received similar training at other pineapple plantations.

Field laborers are specialists in their own right. Although the picking of fruit and removal of weeds by hoe are customarily done in the summer months by inexperienced employees, successful year-round operation depends upon skill at the presumably unskilled tasks of field laborers. Operations such as the removal of shoots for planting and the insertion of plants into the ground require a high degree of coördination gained from supervised training and experience. Much of the mechanical equipment and many of the techniques of use of standard machines are peculiar to pineapple plantations and must be learned. Operators of trucks and other mobile equipment ordinarily come from the ranks of laborers and hold these more highly paid positions only after they have completed a closely supervised course of training. Mechanics and certain other skilled workmen may have had outside training in trade schools. More commonly, however, their training has been received on the plantation.

In-plantation training applies not only to laborers and skilled workmen but also to most supervisory employees. Although they may be engaged with the intent of final assignment to positions of considerable authority, these employees are usually placed first in lesser supervisory posts where they come into close contact with plantation workmen and virtually learn the business "from the ground up."

Plantation policies of home training and promotion to higher-ranking positions encourage occupational mobility. Employees who show promise of developing specialized skills or the ability to direct other men are given the required training when positions are available. Employees may apply at any time for better positions or for training which might enable them to hold such positions. When one or two additional employees are needed for semiskilled or skilled positions, it is customary to select promising persons without any general notice. If the number required is fairly large, selection is made from among aspirants who have responded to a call for volunteers. Salaried supervisory positions may also be filled by former hourly employees, and many non-Haole supervisors have risen from the ranks in this manner.

Direction of plantation work is accomplished through a ramified but clearly defined occupational hierarchy. Personal hierarchies—that is, positions of relative dominance and submission in social relations based upon personal qualities rather than upon occupational status —certainly exist, but they apply only among employees of the same or very similar occupational rank. Relationships of this sort appear to be common among the hourly employees, but rare among the salaried administrative and supervisory employees, who are fewer in number and hold positions on the occupational ladder with many more clearly defined steps.

Personal hierarchies, in any case, do not cut across occupational steps among the supervisory employees. Periodic transfer of supervisory employees to other plantations or business enterprises of the corporation discourages the growth of these relationships. More important is the fact that relations of this sort are discouraged by managerial personnel as inimical to the efficient operation of the plantation. A chain of authority and command such as customarily exists in business concerns is regarded as the only efficient means of operation. A person whose actual role or behavior does not conform with his occupational status is considered a poor employee.

The occupational scale describes in graphic form the irregular pyramidal arrangement common enough in American business concerns, proceeding from one person, the manager, at the apex to a mass of field laborers at the base. Within the outlines of the major pyramid are several minor pyramids—specialized occupational branches which have little contact during the working day with the other elements of the pyramid. The principal component of the major pyramid is employees directly concerned with the raising and transporting of pine-apples. Major subgroups consist of shop personnel who maintain and repair mechanical equipment, and office personnel who are responsible for payroll, cost accounting, and personnel records.

Social distances commonly increase in proportion to differentials in job and pay. By far the greatest gulf lies between the small group of salaried employees, who serve in clerical, administrative, and super-visory capacities, and the large body of employees paid on an hourly basis, who comprise the labor force. With the partial exception of a few young female clerks and typists, most of whom are the wives of employees and do not view their positions as lifetime careers, the social elevation of salaried personnel is far above that of hourly workers. Even these young women, whose earnings are less than those of many hourly workmen, are accorded considerable prestige as salaried white-collar workers. Differences in educational and cultural backgrounds between salaried and hourly employees are so marked that the two groups will be described separately.

HOURLY EMPLOYEES

Of the total of 475 regular employees of the plantation (as of June 8, 1956; see table 1), nearly 90 per cent are employed at hourly rates as laborers and in various semiskilled and skilled capacities. By far the greatest number of the total personnel, approximately 57 per cent, are classified as laborers. An additional 5 per cent hold semiskilled positions paying rates within the scale paid to laborers (included with laborers in table 1). Most of these employees are trainees for higher-paying positions. Approximately 27 per cent are semiskilled and skilled workmen paid at rates exceeding those of laborers. These employees are principally mechanics and operators of trucks and other mechanical equipment. Included in this group are a few welders, carpenters, and other skilled craftsmen required for the maintenance of buildings and equipment.

More than three-fourths of plantation workmen are Filipinos, and nearly all laborers (94 per cent) are Filipinos born in the Philippines. The few Japanese who serve as laborers are, with one exception, im-migrants from Japan who are now well along in years and approaching

TABLE 1

YEAR-ROUND EMPLOYEES, MAUNALOA PLANTATION
(As of June 8, 1956)

Racial-cultural affiliation	Hourly employees — Laborers[a] No.	Laborers[a] Per cent	Semiskilled and skilled No.	Semiskilled and skilled Per cent	Total No.	Total Per cent	Salaried employees No.	Salaried employees Per cent	All employees Total no.	All employees Per cent
Filipino	278 (2)[b]	94.3	80	62.0	358 (2)	84.4	14 (2)	27.4	372 (4)	78.3
Japanese	5 (2)	1.7	23	17.8	28 (2)	6.6	22 (5)	43.1	50 (7)	10.5
Part Hawaiian	8	2.7	12	9.2	20	4.7	3	5.9	23	4.8
Hawaiian	2 (1)	less than 1.0 each	6	4.7	8 (1)	1.9	1	2.0	9 (1)	1.8
Haole	—		1	.8	1	less than 1.0 each	7	13.7	8	1.7
Portuguese	1		2	1.6	3		1	2.0	4	less than 1.0 each
Part Filipino	—		4	3.1	4		1 (1)	2.0	5 (1)	
Chinese	1		—	—	1		2	3.9	3	
Puerto Rican	—		1	.8	1		—	—	1	
Total	295 (5)	100	129	100	424 (5)	100	51 (8)	100	475 (13)	100
Per cent of total hourly employees	69.6[a]		30.4		100					
Per cent of total hourly and salaried employees	62.1[a]		27.2		89.3		10.7			

[a] Includes all employees receiving hourly wages within the range paid to laborers whether so classified or not. Approximately 5 per cent of hourly employees under various classifications are paid at the same rates as laborers.

[b] Figures in parentheses represent female employees who are included with males in figures to the left of parentheses.

the age of retirement. The dozen laborers of other racial-cultural back-grounds are American-born and principally of Hawaiian or part-Hawaiian ancestry.

Maunaloa is exceptional among pineapple plantations in the number of employees of Hawaiian ancestry, a circumstance which reflects racial distribution and special conditions of landownership on the Island of Molokai. As a result of a Territorial program of "rehabilitation" of Hawaiians which granted a number of forty-acre homestead plots on Molokai to persons whose genetic composition was half or more Hawaiian, landowning Hawaiians and part Hawaiians are relatively great in number. Approximately one-fourth of the plantation lands are leased from these homesteaders, and contracts of lease carry the stipulation that the homesteaders receive preference in employment if they meet the standards of work demanded of other employees. As a reflection of the rarity of Hawaiians and part Hawaiians among pineapple plantation personnel, it is said that one Hawaiian pineapple plantation has in its employ a single part-Hawaiian workman, who is referred to with pride as "our Hawaiian."

The relatively small number of males among hourly employees who are not Filipino, Hawaiian, or part Hawaiian are engaged chiefly in semiskilled and skilled occupations. Four women, all over fifty years of age (two Japanese women, a circumstance which is not unusual —but, surprisingly, also one woman of Hawaiian and one of Filipino descent), serve as field laborers, working in crews together with men. These women are said to be given somewhat preferential treatment by their foremen, with the approval of male members of their crews. They might be allowed to work nearest the road when hand-picking fruit so that they need carry heavy loads only short distances, or be given other favors of similar sort. The individual production and earnings of these women, who are paid at a guaranteed hourly rate very slightly less than that of men, are somewhat lower than the average for male laborers. A fifth female hourly employee, a young Filipino woman, is stock clerk in the automotive maintenance shop.

The amount of formal education, which averages 3.4 years of school for all hourly employees (see table 2), is strongly correlated with occupational rank and country of birth. The small number (66) of American-born hourly employees averages 8.8 years of schooling, whereas the much larger number (358) of foreign-born employees averages 2.3 years. The latter circumstance reflects chiefly the educational status of the numerically dominant group, the Filipinos, who average two and one-half years of school as opposed to nearly nine years for other hourly employees. More than 20 per cent of hourly-paid Filipinos declare themselves to be totally illiterate, and approximately 30 per cent claim literacy in one or more Philippine languages but illiteracy in English. Many Filipinos who claim illiteracy, however, appear to have some knowledge of written as well as spoken English, and a small number who have had no formal education declare themselves as literate, a circumstance which does not appear to represent false claims. Nearly all are able to do simple recording of figures and simple addition, accomplishments which are required even among laborers, as individual production figures must be recorded.

TABLE 2

LITERACY AND YEARS OF FORMAL EDUCATION OF HOURLY EMPLOYEES

	Total number	Average years schooling	Number illiterate	Number illiterate in English
Filipino:				
Philippine-born				
Arrived in Hawaii before 1946	262	1.8	87	121
Arrived in Hawaii in 1946 ...	84	3.6	12	16
Hawaii-born	12	9.5	—	—
	358	2.5	99	137
Japanese:				
Japan-born	12	5.5	1	9
Hawaii-born	16	9.5	—	—
	28	7.8	1	9
All others (All American-born) ..	38	8.3	—	—
Total foreign-born	358	2.3	100	146
Total American-born	66	8.8	—	—
All hourly employees	424	3.4	100	146

With the exception of a single illiterate, issei have ordinarily completed at least the six years of compulsory public school attendance required in Japan during their childhood. Of the twelve issei employees, nine claim illiteracy in English. Like other self-declared illiterates, however, some of this number appear to have at least a little knowledge of written English.

The average length of service of hourly employees is thirteen years. Turnover in labor during the early years of the history of the plantation was rapid and, with plateaus and peaks here and there, it has continued to be fairly great until the last decade. Many Filipinos have broken tenure as employees, having severed their employment themselves and returned after absences lasting from several weeks to several years. Some have repeated the process several times. A plantation-wide strike of several weeks in 1937, when many employees found other work, and wartime resignations to take higher-paying defense work in Honolulu represent the periods and occasions of greatest turnover. Increasing mechanization and efficiency since shortly after the end of World War II have lowered needs for labor, and the trend since 1948 has been toward reduction rather than hiring.

Nearly one-fourth of the hourly personnel of 1956 were employed during the period from 1946 to 1948 to replace losses by resignation during the war. Since 1948, however, hiring of regular employees has been confined to a few skilled craftsmen and essential replacements, and many employees have been laid off. The small number of employees lost through retirement or resignation since 1948 are also, in effect, layoffs, because these men were seldom replaced. Hourly workers employed as of 1956 who had entered employment after 1948 totaled only twelve, of whom six were hired in 1949.

Reduction in the number of employees, coming at a time when little work of equal or superior pay was available in Hawaii, has helped to stabilize plantation personnel. Plantation employment has become desirable. Reduction in personnel, carried out at the expense of newer and ordinarily younger employees, has contributed to make the average age of the plantation labor force high. The number of young persons is very small. Only six of the total of 424 regular hourly employees in the summer of 1956 were under thirty years of age. The average age of all hourly employees was forty-three years, and approximately 50 per cent of all hourly personnel were forty-seven years old or older.

Managerial personnel are well aware of the advanced and advancing age of the labor force. No plan of action to meet future problems arising from these circumstances has yet been devised, however, because it is difficult to foresee just what the problems might be. Increased mechanization and increased efficiency in horticultural techniques might drastically reduce needs for labor within the next ten years, but it is difficult to make prognoses at present. In any case, old employees with many years of service are given preferential treatment when it

TABLE 3

AGE OF HOURLY EMPLOYEES

	Number of employees	Cumulative percentage
Age 65 or under	419 [a]	100
Under 60	386	92.1
Under 55	346	82.6
Under 50	278	66.3
Under 45	169	40.3
Under 40	99	23.6
Under 35	63	15.0
Under 30	6	1.4
Under 25	2	.5

[a] Data lacking on five employees, all of middle or advanced middle age.

is necessary to reduce personnel; so the labor force, whatever its size, will doubtless include many aged men for years to come.

A noteworthy characteristic of plantation workmen is the great number of single men among them. Again, this circumstance reflects conditions among the Filipinos rather than among employees of other racial-cultural origins, most of whom are married. When the plantation began operations in 1923, the practice of hiring single men was followed in part to eliminate the expense of providing housing and other facilities for wives and dependents, and in part because the isolation and pioneering conditions of life in western Molokai discouraged men with families from entering employment.

Effectively single male employees (that is, the unmarried, widowers, divorced and separated persons, and married men whose wives do not reside in Hawaii), both salaried and hourly, total over 300 persons, or approximately 65 per cent of the total personnel. The presence of this relatively huge number of wifeless men has important effects on social relations in the plantation community.

TABLE 4

MARITAL STATUS OF MALE FILIPINO HOURLY EMPLOYEES

Married, wives residing in Hawaii	74
Married, wives residing in the Philippines	94
Single	159
Widowers, divorced, separated	31
Total	358

SALARIED EMPLOYEES

Employees on regular monthly salaries, the occupational elite of the plantation, differ markedly in background and attitude from the workmen paid by the hour. The topmost positions are those of manager, assistant manager, and field superintendent (three), transportation superintendent in charge of trucks and other mobile equipment, and personnel superintendent. Other supervisory or administrative positions of importance include those of shop superintendent, office manager, time-study engineers, and field foremen. Agricultural research workers, a registered nurse, and an office staff of clerks, typists, and a secretary round out the total of fifty-one salaried employees.

The largest single category of supervisory employees is that of gang foremen (more commonly called *lunas*, the term of Hawaiian plantation tradition for foremen of this kind), who directly superintend the work of field laborers. Supervisory steps proceed from the *lunas* through two succeeding classes of foremen to the manager and his assistant. Workmen are divided into crews normally not exceeding thirty persons under one *luna*. Unless or until special circumstances make change necessary, a man's assignment to a gang is likely to be permanent. Each crew of field workmen is visited frequently by the various field supervisors, who travel by car from crew to crew, directing their work and inspecting its quality and progress. Unless the nature of the day's work, such as planting, disperses field laborers of a single gang over a wide area, they are normally under constant supervision, channeled through the succeeding orders of command.

Employees of Japanese extraction outnumber any other racial-cultural group among the salaried employees. All presently employed Japanese supervisory personnel are nisei. They hold good positions, with considerable authority, but generally of second echelon. Filipinos make the second largest group of salaried employees, but comprise only a small part of the total number of Filipino personnel. Except for one female clerk, salaried Filipinos monopolize and are limited to the lowest of the field supervisory positions, as *lunas* in charge of workmen who are almost all Filipinos. The best positions are held by Haoles, who are third in number among salaried employees. Scattered about in various capacities are the few supervisory employees of Chinese, Portuguese, and Cosmopolitan backgrounds. (See table 1.)

Supervisory employees average eleven years of formal schooling. Excluding *lunas,* whose formal schooling averages about five years, virtually all salaried employees have finished high school. Twelve persons have attended college or university, and nine hold one or more college degrees. Haoles are ordinarily college graduates, as are the younger and more newly employed of the Japanese. For many years it has been a policy to give marked preference to persons with college degrees in suitable fields of specialization. Most of the Haoles engaged for field administrative positions hold degrees granted by agricultural colleges.

The plantation workday ordinarily begins at 6:30 in the morning and ends at 3:00. Mechanics, clerks, and other specialists whose tasks are done within the settlement proceed by themselves to their places of work. Field workers gather at the "turn-out stations," one at Maunaloa and one at Hoolehua, and are transported to the fields by truck. For the stated reason that they are unable to sleep longer, a substantial number of workmen arrive early, sometimes as much as thirty minutes before the time of departure, to chat with friends.

The normal work week for hourly employees is five eight-hour days, Monday through Friday. During a fourteen-week period at the height of summer harvest, the union contract allows a six-day week. Hourly employees receive 50 per cent additional pay for all work above these maxima.

Rain puts a halt to all field work. Any precipitation beyond light showers (fairly common despite the unimpressive total annual rainfall) renders the field roads extremely dangerous or impassable for vehicles. Field employees also strongly dislike to work in the rain. The fleeting showers so common in Hawaii—mere suggestions of rain falling spottily here and there through the sunlight and lasting a few seconds or minutes—are very common and tolerated, but any flurry sufficient to wet the field roads ordinarily drives workmen back to their homes. Raincoats are sometimes taken along when rain threatens, but they are uncomfortably warm and restricting garments in which to work. Even employees in fields adjacent to the community, engaged in tasks which might be continued during light rains, cease work for the day when there seems to be any likelihood of a modest wetting. Because rainfall is often extremely localized and crews of workmen are dispersed, it is a common event for two or three crews to return to camp, while the remaining men, working in fields untouched by rain, continue through the day. Heavy winter rains may render field roads impassable for days and thus effectively stop all field operations until the roadways have dried. To most field workmen, rain provides a welcome excuse for not working.

Lunch is ordinarily taken in the field by all employees from the rank of gang foreman down. Field supervisors, who move about by automobile, and personnel whose duties are chiefly in the community ordinarily lunch at home or, less commonly, in the community restaurant. Depending upon the pressure of work, higher supervisors may take an hour or more for the noon meal. The thirty-minute lunch period of field workers—kept short at their request so that work may end earlier—is one of conviviality. A crew of twenty-odd workmen ordinarily gathers in two or three groups. Sitting or squatting on the ground in a circle, they share some of the contents of their aluminum lunch buckets. In addition to rice, a workman might thus partake of many different kinds of food, including spaghetti, macaroni, chop suey, and various Philippine dishes of cooked vegetables and meat.

Few employees take fruit or sweets into the field, and they are unimportant in the Filipino diet. Fresh pineapples are, however, eaten rather frequently in the field. A pineapple is quickly prepared for consumption by a few slashes with a knife, and usually only the most desirable parts are eaten. (Pineapples tend to increasing sweetness as one proceeds from surface to core and from crown to base and one may choose the sweet or the tart.) Each worker carries water in a wine bottle or canteen, but on hot days during the harvest season coöperative truck drivers might bring wine jugs filled with water for communal use to replenish individual supplies.

The noon meal is viewed as a time of pleasure, and exclusion from one of the lunch groups—which is rare unless a worker is among the few who eat sandwiches or other foods not easily shared—constitutes a serious form of ostracism. No other fixed periods of rest are taken. Short normal interruptions caused by such necessary activities as adjusting mechanical equipment or moving it to another area occur frequently throughout the day. If a man is engaged in tasks wherein no interruptions of this kind occur, he simply stops to rest when he feels tired.

Work ceases promptly at 3:00, when field employees clamber aboard waiting trucks for transport back to the turn-out station. Normal activities which follow are a bath, dinner, several hours spent in individual pursuits, and early retirement. Soon after nine o'clock most lights are out.

In a normal year about 250 days of work are offered to field employees. During the summer harvest, overtime hours may run to a considerable number. When fruit matures faster than it can be harvested during an eight-hour day, it is customary to operate two shifts, the first and larger shift engaging in all normal plantation operations as well as harvesting. The second shift, much smaller in size, is composed only of harvesting crews and the workmen needed to service equipment and transport fruit from the fields. Double shifts, which entail long hours of work for many of the supervisory employees, are avoided unless the pressure of rapidly ripening fruit makes them unavoidable, and they ordinarily last no more than a few weeks of the year.

Few field laborers work every day that work is offered. Failure to report for work has always been a serious problem to Hawaiian plantations hiring Filipino workmen. Work for work's sake appears clearly to be no Filipino ideal. Well-defined rules exist to prevent unexcused absences, and equally well-known if not formally defined ways of circumventing the rules also exist. To qualify for employee benefits such as paid vacations and eligibility under the pension plan, hourly employees must work at least 1,600 hours annually, or approximately 200 days.

Absenteeism is of sufficient importance to be dealt with in the union contract. According to the regulations, a single unexcused absence results in a warning, the second entails an enforced layoff of one day, and the third results in discharge. Employees may be excused from work to attend to personal affairs, and such excused leaves of absence are extremely common. The simplest and most common way of gaining an authorized rest of a single day or a few days, however, is to "go Hawaii sick." Employees who have failed to report for work appear before the plantation nurse to declare themselves as sick. By far the most common and efficient form of "Hawaii sick" is a headache. It entails only the reporting of a headache, the registering of a name and employee number, and the swallowing of two aspirin tablets. Other ailments, such as a stomach-ache, might require distasteful medication or more lengthy examination. The registered nurse, thoroughly experienced in matters of this kind, serves as a screening device to separate the genuinely sick from the "Hawaii sick," and at the same time provides an officially acceptable excuse for a day of rest or amusement for dissemblers.

Although the practice of disguising absences by medical excuses is well known to everyone and causes a large economic loss to the corporation, no effective means of ending it have been devised. The demeanor of the employee usually labels his intent very clearly, but there is always the possibility that he might actually be sick.

Absenteeism is, however, much decreased over former times. To be retained in permanent employment, a man must be reasonably efficient and must conform fairly well to a routine of day-in and day-out work. In the three decades of the plantation's history, thousands of employees have entered employment and have subsequently resigned or have been discharged. Only those temperamentally suited to plantation work and plantation community life remain.

Hawaiians and part Hawaiians have the reputation of being unsatisfactory because they cannot be relied upon to work regularly throughout the year. The relatively large number at Maunaloa constitutes a very small proportion of the total Hawaiian and part-Hawaiian population of the island. They are "good" employees who have met the demands of production and regularity of work, and are the few survivors of many who have at some time been employed.

Reduction in personnel as the result of mechanization since World War II has been powerful as a selective force. Barring considerations of length of employment, which have sometimes served to retain workmen of long service who might be less efficient than newer employees, reduction has been at the expense of the least reliable and least efficient. Even the dullest employee is aware of the trend, and he knows also that other work which will provide as high earnings and as many benefits is not abundant. Voluntary resignation has doubtless been very important in eliminating those who do not adapt easily to plantation demands.

Earnings of regular hourly employees during 1955 averaged approximately $3,000, a sum which left most employees with considerable money for purposes other than food, lodging, and clothing. Few workmen are actually paid the official hourly rate of their job classification. Instead, this rating represents a guaranteed minimum. The plantation has long maintained a policy whereby most employees are paid on the basis of production rather than upon hours worked. In the Old Stone Age of this policy, it was referred to simply as "contract" or piece-work. Unit rates were set for operations such as hoeing, plant removal, planting, and picking, and employees were paid upon the basis of individual or group units of production as recorded by themselves, by time-keepers, or by foremen. Another Old Stone Age working policy, called by the Hawaiian name *hanapau*, set a reasonable work allotment for the day and employees might work at greater than normal speed to finish the day in less than eight hours.

In modern postwar dress the successor to these policies is called the "incentive program" or "industrial engineering." Several specialists, trained in time-and-motion studies, are employed to set standards of production for plantation operations, field or shop, which involve more than a few men. Standards of field work are set for small segments of fields and changed frequently because of the many variable factors such as density of plant or weed growth and density of harvestable fruit. In 1956 standards applied to nearly 90 per cent of annual hours worked by hourly employees, and plans for the future called for the setting of standards to cover additional types of duties.

Despite the efforts of the company to explain the means by which standards are set, the actual techniques of the time-and-motion studies are poorly understood or incomprehensible to most field employees. All are keenly aware, however, of the rates applying to the work they are performing at any given day and hour, and know very quickly whether or not the unit standard for the day will allow them to make earnings above the guaranteed minimum. "Good" standards are an incentive to production greater than normal, and "loose" standards—those which are very lenient—serve as an even greater stimulus to increase production. When standards are "tight," the workmen make no attempt to exert themselves, but rely upon the guaranteed minimum hourly wage.

A rather large proportion of the earnings of nearly all hourly employees consists of bonus pay. An exceptionally fast and efficient field laborer, especially a skilled planter who is able to work at his own speed, unimpeded by others, may earn annual wages exceeding those of semiskilled and skilled employees paid at higher hourly rates. For the unusually energetic and skillful, premium earnings may amount to as much as 30 per cent of annual wages. Few employees would favor abandonment of the incentive program. On the negative side, as far as management is concerned, piecework encourages slipshod work and the falsifying by employees of records of production. Guarding against behavior of this sort is one of the responsibilities of gang foremen and higher supervisors.

Nearly 90 per cent of hourly employees are members of the local branch of the International Longshoremen's and Warehousemen's Union, which spread throughout much of Hawaiian industry during the war and embraced Maunaloa plantation in 1946. By 1947 most of the plantation workmen had become union members. The plantation remains, however, open shop. Nonunion members state that little pressure is exerted upon them to join the union. The common sanctions of ridicule and ostracism to induce conformity are not strong, for, after many years of association, one does not easily turn against his friends.

Reasons for failing to join the union are varied. A few employees, members of the Filipino Federation of America and Jehovah's Witnesses, are prohibited from union membership by religious beliefs. In ratio to their total number, Japanese are the most poorly represented as union members. A few issei express the sentiment that they feel bound by loyalty to "the company," and entering the union would somehow constitute a breach of loyalty. Some persons do not want to pay the monthly dues of $5 which membership entails. According to provisions of the contract between the union and the corporation, dues are deducted from the wages of employees and transmitted to the union. It is safe to assume that if dues were not collected in this manner but were left to individual employees and union representatives, delinquency would be common.

Union membership is, however, looked upon as desirable by most hourly employees, and unionization of the plantation has affected everyone, at work and in community life. A written contract binds both the union and the corporation to fairly clear-cut regulations and procedures. Officials of the plantation corporation headquarters in Honolulu are kept well informed of union activities. Minor disputes over interpretation of the contract have arisen frequently, and the course of their settlement has often been stormy. Most issues concerning money or wages have resulted in the company bowing to union demands. If, however, demands are regarded by local and Honolulu plantation officials as matters of principle, their opposition may be strong and dogged.

Union affairs of the plantation local are handled by a single salaried representative of the union, who serves for the Island of Molokai. Union representatives in the employ of the plantation include five officers and twenty-seven stewards, presided over by a stewards' chairman, each of whom is elected for a term of one year. Each field crew of laborers ordinarily has two stewards among its members, and all other occupational groups include one or more stewards. Reports and issues are channeled from stewards to the stewards' chairman to the officers, and are finally referred to the outside union representative for consultation and action. Most employees appear to be reluctant to serve as union representatives, and officers of the union generally serve for only one term.

There has been much argument concerning the disposition of the union dues collected locally and the merits and operations of the local union, but no one would deny that its influence has been great. To the majority of field employees, who have little knowledge of national affairs, the union represents personal security, a means of promoting their own welfare and of recourse against injustice. The common opinion among employees of managerial rank to field laborers is that the union has brought benefits to all, union members and nonmembers, paid by the hour or on salary. Characteristically, salaried employees, who are excluded from union membership, ally themselves with "management" and are opposed to the union, despite expressed opinions that they too have derived benefits as concomitants of benefits received by members. And, characteristically, hourly employees view unionization as good from their standpoint, but believe that "the company doesn't like it."

Unionization of the plantation has resulted in a gingerly attitude on the part of managerial and supervisory employees in relations with other employees. Some of the workmen state that supervisory personnel, in the old days, used to "bawl the hell out of" hourly employees for poor performances or other real or fancied offenses, but that they no longer do so for fear of union action. A more nearly accurate statement is that politeness and consideration have steadily increased in supervisor-workman relations since the rough-and-ready days of the infancy of the plantation. A quick temper and rough speech on the part of a supervisor had been considered serious failings long before the arrival of the union.

Plantation personnel receive all the benefits commonly extended by American industrial concerns. Employees are entitled to paid vacations varying in length according to their tenure. In addition to medical treatment for industrial accidents as required by law, the corporation supports a medical plan which provides for the treatment of nonindustrial injury or illness of employees and dependents. A retirement plan, operated at no cost to personnel, applies to all employees. Facilities are provided for the recreation and welfare of the men and their families (see chap. iii).

An important consideration in plantation affairs is the fact that the Maunaloa plantation is not autonomous. It is but one of three Hawaiian plantations controlled by a corporation which has many similar enterprises in other parts of the world. Policies and objectives come to the plantation from the corporation management in the continental United States by way of the Hawaiian headquarters in Honolulu, and they are modified in Honolulu and on the plantation to meet local conditions. The fact that corporation interests are not focused directly on the plantation community or even on Hawaii has favored a strong commercial feeling and inhibited personalized relationships among employees. Maunaloa plantation is frequently visited by managerial personnel from the headquarters in Honolulu as well as by architects, engineers, chemists, and other professional employees of the corporation who serve its Hawaiian division. Less frequently, managerial personnel from the mainland come on visits of inspection. In recent years the highest-ranking supervisory employees of the Hawaiian plantations have sometimes been asked to attend the winter training programs conducted on the mainland for such corporation employees. Extended as privileges offered only to the most promising executives, and providing in addition an expense-paid change of scene, these invitations are eagerly accepted.

The annual round of plantation work is one of intense activity in summer, tapering to a relatively slack period in winter. Attempts are made to distribute work throughout the year, but the tendency of the crop toward seasonal maturation makes them only partly successful. A factor strongly favoring seasonal peaks of work is that pineapple maturing in the summer months are of finer quality than those maturing in the cooler periods of the year. During the winter more attention is given to the repair and maintenance of equipment and to training programs for supervisory and administrative employees. Meetings are held on rainy days and other slack times to instruct these employees in safety procedures, desirable patterns of relationship with subordinates, the incentive program, and other matters.

Adult male seasonal employees do not enter importantly into plantation life. Drawn from outside communities, they generally commute by private automobile. Single male adults may occupy quarters within the community, but the number of seasonal employees who do so has gradually decreased to a very small figure.

The many high-school students who compose a large part of the seasonal force are almost entirely sons and daughters of Molokai residents and principally the children of regular plantation employees. According to Territorial law they must be at least sixteen years old and can work only five days a week. Hourly rates paid them are slightly below those of adults, but premium rates are the same. The plantation has always followed a policy of giving special attention to the welfare of its seasonal minors. Girls, and usually also boys, are placed in separate crews, often supervised by a local schoolteacher who wishes summer employment. A recreation program, including dances and sports, is provided for them, under the direction of the personnel superintendent. Most of the boys and girls view the summer of work as a profitable and rather pleasant experience.

III | *The Community*

Approximately 78 per cent of the employees of the plantation live in the community of Maunaloa. Most of the 22 per cent who live outside work in the Hoolehua fields, ten or more miles from Maunaloa. As of June 8, 1956, the residents of Maunaloa totaled 807, of whom 39 were adults not employed by the plantation, and the spouses, children, and other dependents of these persons. Included in the latter category are the staff of the community grammar school, several employees of the two stores, the postmaster, a restaurant cook, and a barber.

The population of permanent residents is augmented by a floating and officially unsanctioned population of twenty to thirty persons. Included in this group are a handful of professional gamblers of Filipino

TABLE 5

RACIAL-CULTURAL COMPOSITION OF POPULATION OF MAUNALOA

	Adult male	Adult female	Children under 18	Total
Filipino	306 (224) [a]	54	124	484
Japanese	39 (8)	35 (2)	60	134
Haole	8 (1)	11 (2)	11	30
Puerto Rican	1	3	6	10
Portuguese	2	3	3	8
Chinese	4 (1)	1	—	5
Hawaiian	—	2	—	2
Cosmopolitan	7	24 (4)	103	134
Total	367 (234)	133 (8)	307	807

[a] Figures in parentheses represent effectively single persons—the unmarried, widows, widowers, the divorced and separated, and all married persons whose spouses do not reside at Maunaloa.

extraction and a few women of various or mixed ancestries who, if their residence continues for some months, may be given the unofficial title of common-law wives. Other floaters are much more difficult to label. Some of them, adult males who are friends of employees and become their unofficial dependents, are referred to by managerial employees simply as "hangers-on." On paydays (twice monthly) and for several days afterward the community may be visited by female vendors who sell gaudy "aloha" shirts, other items of masculine clothing, and cosmetics to male Filipinos. Floaters are difficult to detect unless they stay for some time, and no concerted effort is made to remove them unless they cause disturbance. Swelling the population at any given time are also a number of visiting relatives of employees.

The racial-cultural composition of the community differs in some respects from that of the plantation personnel (see tables 1 and 3), since many wives, and thus many children, differ in ethnic affiliation from their husbands and fathers. Nearly all Hawaiians and part Hawaiians work in the Hoolehua fields and do not live at Maunaloa. Hawaiian heredity is very uncommon among adult males of the community.

Single Filipinos are common on sugar and pineapple plantations, but the Maunaloa statistics doubtless represent an extreme, based partly on the former plantation practice of favoring single men in employment. Seldom have there been more than two or three unmarried young women. Perhaps more remarkable than the unbalanced ratio between adult males and females is its relative unimportance as a source of serious discord. This was not so in the past, when sexual jealousy was the most common cause of strife in the community, but dissension of this kind involving physical violence has become infrequent.

Although adult Cosmopolitan employees in residence are few, the community is nevertheless remarkable in the number of members of mixed racial and cultural provenience. The Cosmopolitan population of Maunaloa, like that of other pineapple plantations, differs in its composition from that of the Territory of Hawaii as a whole, and the proportion of Cosmopolitans to non-Cosmopolitans is rather lower than that of the Territory. This circumstance reflects the small number of part Hawaiians, who compose by far the largest category of Cosmopolitans in Hawaii but who do not frequently take plantation employment. The majority of Maunaloa Cosmopolitans are part-Filipino children.

In physical conformation the community of Maunaloa is irregular. Several blocks of houses and other buildings flank the main thoroughfare to form the central part of the settlement, and a single line of dwellings marches up the hill. The plantation office, which once served as the community hospital, may be described as the heart of both the plantation and the community. It houses an office staff of ten persons, the field administrative and supervisory personnel, and a medical dispensary. A company physician uses the dispensary for consultation and examination of patients. A second doctor, who is in part-time attendance, has a separate office.

The public buildings comprise two rival general merchandise stores, which carry groceries as their principal stock, the post office, a small restaurant, a moving picture house, a service station for privately owned automobiles, a combined poolroom and barbershop, the tiny office of the visiting dentist, the headquarters of the local federal credit union, and several buildings of the primary school. A low wooden structure is used for community affairs, such as dances for the young people among the seasonal employees and the inoculation of children under the county health program; two smaller buildings are the Japanese clubhouse and the Filipino clubhouse. There is a tennis court which is seldom used. A television and radio sales and repair shop is operated after working hours by one of the employees, and a quonset hut houses a laundry and dry-cleaning establishment. The Catholic church is the lone religious edifice of the settlement.

The residential community lies on sloping ground and is divided into three major areas, bearing standard but unofficial names which connote important social distinctions. On the lowest level is the group of dwellings known as the Filipino camp, which houses most of the Filipino employees, single and married. Single men usually occupy the least desirable houses at the lower edge of the Filipino camp. Dormitories and communal messes formerly existed for single men, but they now live in dwellings intended originally for families. The small number of single men who are not of Filipino extraction are scattered about in other areas of the community.

Separated from the Filipino camp by the main street and lying at a higher elevation are the blocks of houses known as the Japanese camp, which now includes many Filipino families and other persons of non-Japanese extraction. Most Japanese employees live in houses at the upper margins of this division of the settlement. No Japanese lives in the Filipino camp; it would be difficult to induce a Japanese to do so.

The lower extremities of the third and most desirable residential area

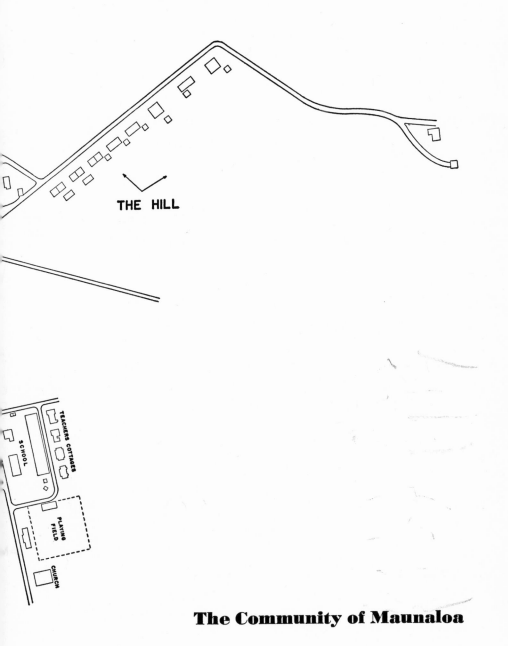

THE HILL

SCHOOL

TEACHERS COTTAGES

PLAYING FIELD

CHURCH

The Community of Maunaloa

lie above the Filipino camp, on the same level as the Japanese camp but separated from it by the main thoroughfare. Dwellings of this group form a line, forked into two tines at the bottom and merging into a single file broken by sections of pineapple fields as one proceeds upward and away from the main settlement. This area, too, bears a popular name, "The Hill," an appellation whose meaning is not strictly geographical. Alternate but less common names are "Nob Hill" and "Snob Hill." "The Hill" is sometimes used to refer only to the uppermost dwellings, which include the homes of the highest plantation officials. The forked area, which lies at a lower level, adjacent to the Japanese camp, and in no physical sense resembles a hill, is sometimes called "The Hill" because it is the site of the homes of important plantation supervisors. The least desirable houses in this area are occupied by employees holding minor positions; these homes and their occupants are somehow understood to be excluded in generic references to "The Hill."

Nearly all the buildings are twenty years old or older. Since 1938 only a few houses on The Hill, modern structures of cinder-block construction, have been built. One of these serves as a guesthouse for visitors from the Honolulu headquarters and other official guests. All the other houses are of light wooden construction. All have modern plumbing and electric water heaters.

Most plantation employees live in cramped quarters. Their small four- or five-room houses are set close together in monotonous blocks bounded by narrow dirt roads. Dust raised by the passage of automobiles along the unsurfaced roads increases the ugliness of the yards and the exteriors of dwellings.

Some householders make no attempt to beautify their homes, and leave them surrounded by raw and dusty red earth, but most dwellings occupied by families have hedges or scattered plantings of hardy shrubs such as hibiscus and croton, and the Norfolk Island pines planted along the roadways of the two camps years ago by the plantation do much to relieve the shortage of continually green vegetation. Here and there in both camps, especially at houses occupied by Japanese employees, are small green oases of shrubs, mauve Vanda orchids, and other colorful blossoming plants. Grounds about the homes of supervisory employees are much larger than those of hourly employees, and tend to be given more attention. After heavy rains, the lawns surrounding houses on The Hill may be quite handsome until the lack of water causes them to revert to their more common semiparched condition. Rows of eucalyptus trees have been planted near the yards on The Hill. Unwatered and wind-torn, these straggling growths contain dead and leafless branches.

Single Filipinos frequently plant fruit trees and vegetables in both back and front yards, and many householders raise a few vegetables. Scraggly wind-damaged papaya, banana, and avocado trees are common. Larger plots around the peripheries of the Japanese and Filipino camps are available to employees. Here men with families may raise sweet potatoes and, with the protection of windbreaks, various kinds of beans and other vegetables. In dollars and cents this horticulture is of slight importance, but it does provide vegetables fresher than are available by purchase, and, for Filipinos, is the means of obtaining products important in the traditional Philippine diet which are not raised commercially in Hawaii.

A second form of home husbandry, the raising of laying hens, is more common, but this, too, is of slight economic importance. Fresh eggs are always expensive in Hawaii, where chicken feed must be imported. To ensure a supply of fresh and somewhat cheaper eggs as well as an occasional bird for the table, many employees, including supervisory personnel, raise chickens. A few persons also raise rabbits for the table.

Community members give more attention to fowl of a different sort. Fighting cocks, customarily called "chickens," are raised by Philippine-born Filipinos. The population of mature fighting cocks of the community, estimated at 1,000, greatly exceeds the human population. A formidable chorus of crowing at dawn operates for many as a reminder to rise and begin the day's work. Because of their unsightliness, pens for gamecocks are concentrated, by official order, in two areas at the lower margins of the community. Composed of wire and odds and ends of galvanized iron and boards, the haphazardly built structures are eyesores which give a false impression of backwoods poverty.

Although exteriors of houses are often dust-streaked and uninviting, a high standard of cleanliness is maintained within family dwellings. Uniformity prevails in furnishing and décor. The small living room characteristically contains upholstered chairs, a table lamp, a television and (or) radio set, and a couch or sofa. Rattan furniture is popular, as are Hawaiian-made chairs and sofas with brightly varnished wooden frames and cushions covered with tropical flower prints. The walls may be adorned with cheap, highly colored prints of hibiscus, bird-of-paradise, and other tropical flowers. Framed enlargements of family photographs, sometimes so tinted and retouched that their subjects are hardly recognizable, are treasured ornaments. Floors are frequently covered with linoleum or pandanus mats.

Most families cook on electric ranges, which have replaced the hand-pumped kerosene and gas stoves that were in use before World War II. Single men still use kerosene stoves. Electric refrigerators are standard equipment for both families and single men.

Homes of supervisory employees on The Hill vary greatly in size and quality, according to occupational rank and the size of the family. They range from admittedly ugly and architecturally poor structures to well-built and attractive homes. Furnishings are much like those of homes in the continental United States except for the accent on "tropical" furniture.

Housing is closely linked with occupational status; the better one's job the better one's house. Convenience and individual preference, however, may determine the question of housing. A supervisory employee might prefer a house at a lower level than The Hill proper, but he would not of his own choice live in a house outside the area occupied by his peers and superiors.

Rents are low, ranging from $4.15 a month for a single man sharing a bedroom with another man to $72.00 a month for the largest and finest house. Rent for single men averages less than $10 a month. Most married hourly employees with families pay rentals of $24 for a four-room house or $32.50 for a five-room house. These charges, which average less than 10 per cent of earnings, are considered high by workmen, although they know that comparable facilities in Honolulu rent at several times the price. Houses in the camps are seldom unoccupied, however, for more than a few days.

For most hourly employees the cost of living is low. Virtually all commodities and services except housing are expensive because Hawaii produces little but sugar, pineapples, and some cattle, and must import nearly all other goods. Prices of commodities on Molokai exceed those prevailing in Honolulu because transshipment from Honolulu is expensive. For hourly employees, at least, the cost of living is nevertheless generally low if expenditures are confined to necessities. Complete medical care is provided at a very modest fee; and expenses for clothing are low because of the warm climate and the nature of plantation work and life. Although food is expensive, the diet of hourly employees consists mainly of rice, which is relatively inexpensive. Thrifty hourly employees who do not indulge in gambling or other extravagances may easily save money, and many do so.

Thrift in domestic affairs and the saving of money—which are not necessarily concomitants—vary with cultural background and occupation: the Japanese are the most provident and the Filipinos the least provident in this respect. Unlike Honolulu or any other independent town or city of Hawaii, Maunaloa "has money," in the sense that all its residents have steady and assured sources of income. No person or family is poverty-stricken except through extravagance, mismanagement, or unusual misfortune.

Savings of most employees are in the form of bank savings and checking accounts. Many employees have shares in the local federal credit union, which extends a large number of loans, especially for the purchase of automobiles and household appliances. Banking is occasionally done by mail directly with Honolulu banks. Most persons, however, use the local branch of a Honolulu bank, which consists of a cashbox, a set of records, and a lone part-time representative who holds brief banking hours in the plantation office twice weekly after he has finished his day's work as a regular clerical employee of the plantation. Some single Filipinos, older men, are said to keep large sums of cash on their persons or secreted in their dwellings, but probably few actually do so.

Successful gamblers are said to keep money on their persons because no other means of retaining it are available to them without incurring penalty. Investment of large sums of money in bank accounts, government bonds, real estate, or any other kind of property is regarded as dangerous because these investments may come to the attention of the Internal Revenue Service. The apprehension several years ago of one successful gambler of the community who had invested his winnings (reported variously as $5,000 to $20,000) in this way and was subsequently fined heavily remains fresh in the minds of men who gamble.

Few ways exist to augment incomes above those earned in plantation employment. With the aid of other members of their families, a very few employees operate a private business—the automobile service station and the television, radio, and appliance shop at Maunaloa, and a poolroom at Kaunakakai. Other part-time sources of income include the local agency for a Honolulu bank, the operation of little-used taxis and of booking agencies at Maunaloa for the two airlines serving the island, occasional vending of fresh fish, and the sale of food and drink at cock-fights. Housewives may engage in domestic work for Haole families and do occasional dressmaking, but these are rarely full-time occupations. Some persons occasionally sell eggs or garden produce to the community stores.

This listing seems impressive, but the actual income gained from subsidiary occupations is usually small. Most housewives are unwilling to work for others. Seasonal employment at field work is available to them, but few women of today would consider it.

Attempts—perhaps better called hopes—to augment incomes by activities of quite a different order are, however, extremely common. Motives of the many Filipino men who gamble undoubtedly include the desire for gain, but few except professional gamblers are winners.

Maunaloa children attend primary school and kindergarten in a group of county-owned buildings located above the Japanese camp. All except one are old and architecturally in no way superior to the worst of the corporation-owned buildings. Extensive playgrounds, equipped with swings, slides, and other recreational devices, and an athletic field complete the school equipment. There are three teachers, a teacher-principal, a cafeteria manager, a secretary, and a janitor. The teachers live in dilapidated houses owned and poorly maintained by the county. In compensation for their poor quality, token rents of a few dollars are charged.

Schoolteachers, who are very guarded in their speech, state that there are no noticeable differences in deportment, interest in school subjects, and marks received among the children of varying cultural and biological strains who make up the student body. Only the teacher who is permanently leaving the community is willing to make qualitative judgments on the progress of Maunaloa students as compared with students of mainland schools. Mainland-raised supervisory employees regard their school as distinctly inferior to those of the mainland, but "no worse than other Hawaiian schools and better than some." Much greater concern is felt about high-school training (locally available in only one outside community of the island). It has long been the custom not only for Haole parents but also for many Japanese to send their children to Maui or Oahu for further schooling after they have completed the primary grades.

The teaching staff customarily includes one or more Haole teachers raised and trained on the mainland. Turnover among these teachers, who are principally young people coming to Hawaii in search of adventure, is usually rapid. After one or two years they may take positions in less isolated communities or return to the mainland. Others on the staff are Hawaii-born and of various racial backgrounds. Their tenure is likely to be greater.

Teachers report that discipline is not a problem, and that in this respect the teacher's life is far more pleasant at Maunaloa than in the public schools of Honolulu. Truancy is rare. A parent-teacher association holds regular and fairly well attended meetings at which mothers are more in evidence than fathers, and parents of Japanese descent are most strongly represented. The plantation corporation provides transportation and other encouragement for athletic events and graduation ceremonies. All school affairs are fairly well attended by parents. As a democratic institution which cuts across social boundaries, the school is probably the most effective single social binder in a community which otherwise has little social cohesion and few pervading ties except employment.

The most common form of speech in the community is substandard English, phonetically if not also grammatically and lexically variant. Phonetically standard American speech of any general or regional variety used on the mainland is extremely rare except among Haoles. A good number of the Hawaii-born, including schoolteachers, regard themselves as speaking "good" English undistinguished from that of the continental United States, but certain differences in phonetic values and patterns of intonation render their speech almost instantly identifiable as Hawaiian English. Rarely, the individual from the mainland insensibly adopts the Hawaiian phonetic patterns. Commonly, Haole children pick them up from playmates at school and also from teachers.

The expression "Pidgin English" is used by Haoles in conversation with other Haoles to designate the phonetically variant but otherwise essentially mainland variety of speech. The expression is used by everyone to indicate markedly deviant and substandard English which includes many Hawaiian words and many distinctive forms and usages of English words. Pidgin English is the lingua franca of the working day, and most hourly employees speak only this kind of English. Except when the intent is to be jocular, persons who speak standard American English are usually careful to avoid the use of Pidgin when addressing persons who understand the socially more highly rated speech.

Pidgin English includes many Hawaiian words used throughout the Territory and also other Hawaiian words, associated with agriculture, which are peculiar to plantations and rural Hawaii. Very few terms derived from languages other than English and Hawaiian are included. Among these are *kaukau* (food; to eat), said to be derived from Cantonese, and the Japanese word *bangō* (number, of a series), officially called "employee number," a numeral which is assigned to each hourly employee and which appears on production, payroll, and personnel records. A few Japanese and Philippine words, principally insulting and scatological terms, may be fairly well known, but they are not considered to be components of Pidgin. Obscene English words are comprehended by everyone.

Much of the distinctiveness of Hawaiian Pidgin comes from phonetic values and unusual usages of common English words and phrases. Familiar examples are "too much" (very), "planty" (plenty—meaning "many" or "very"), and "stop" (to be present; e.g., "Him no stop" He is not here). "Da kine" (the kind) is the most versatile expression of all, perhaps best equated with "that way" or "the thing," the phrase depends upon context for its numerous meanings, which include "to be in love" ("He's da kine for her"), "to be in menses" ("She's da kine"), or any of a variety of attitudes and traits of personality.

Pidgin may be used to express in very few syllables the equivalent of much longer English sentences. A conversation between a field supervisor and a *luna* might consist of but two syllables, "Git?" (get) and the affirmative reply "Git!" or the negative "No git!" This exchange might mean, "Have you found many good slips [for planting] in this field?" with replies of "Yes, a lot," or "No, not very many."

Many usages of English which one hears—Hawaiian rather than local, as no distinctive local speech exists—go far beyond the boundaries of what is ordinarily regarded as Pidgin and might instead be called Hawaiian English. In characteristic speech, for example, women do not "have babies" and children are seldom "born." These ideas are conveyed by the expression "give birth," which is apparently treated as a compound verb: "When my mother gave birth to me"; "She's going to give birth in three months"; "My mother gave birth to five children."

The exchange of simple thoughts on everyday subjects is usually possibly even between the Haole supervisor least skilled in the use of Pidgin English and the Filipino or Japanese least competent in English. For lengthy conversations on unfamiliar subjects, Pidgin often fails as a lingua franca and it is necessary to use an interpreter.

Filipinos, who are seldom credited with intellectual achievement, are the polyglots of the community. Most foreign-born Filipinos speak two Philippine dialects, Ilocano and Tagalog, and some know additional Philippine tongues. Many Filipinos speak fairly fluent English containing varying proportions of Hawaiian Pidgin. Some older men and women have a little knowledge of Spanish. The probable extreme is represented by a middle-aged Filipino who handles English with ease and who claims to know eleven Philippine languages in addition to Spanish.

A second lingua franca is in common but not general use among Filipinos only. Tagalog, the official language of the Philippines, is the native language of a small number of employees, and is a secondary language, learned in school in the Philippines, of the majority of Filipino employees who have had formal schooling.

It is difficult to estimate the knowledge of English possessed by older Filipinos and the few old Japanese who claim no knowledge of the language. Speaking only their native languages and Hawaiian Pidgin, they may nevertheless understand a good deal of English. It is commonly stated by supervisory employees that these men understand English "when they want to."

Employees of Portuguese extraction, who represent the second and third generation of Portuguese born in Hawaii, seldom know the language of their antecedents. The few Chinese of the community may remember Cantonese learned during childhood, but they seldom use it. Japanese is often spoken by issei in conversation with one another, as are Philippine languages among Filipinos, but when these persons are the parents of Hawaii-born children they tend to speak English even among their peers. The first language of nisei and sansei is English.

Competence in English is a source of pride. Proficiency also confers social prestige, and, at least among foreign-born employees of middle age and older, the degree of proficiency is strongly if not precisely correlated with hierarchical social placement. The trend has long been toward increasing use of English and the gradual disappearance of Pidgin English.

Conditions of health are excellent except so far as employees have brought infirmities or predispositions to infirmities with them. Sickness is of highest incidence among the Filipinos, perhaps because of practices of nurture and sanitation during their childhood in the Philippines, and also because their diet, especially that of the single men, is less conducive to good health. In the history of the plantation a number of cases of tuberculosis have been detected among employees, who have received treatment in Territorial sanatoriums. Tuberculosis has been confined almost entirely to the foreign-born. Venereal disease has long been almost nonexistent in the community and on the island. Island physicians, who are required by law to notify the local office of the Territorial Department of Health of all new cases of venereal disease, have reported only one new case in the past five years. Maunaloa children look unusually healthy, an impression which the plantation medical staff confirms.

The people of Maunaloa are well favored in circumstances encouraging good health. Sanitary conditions are excellent; the climate is dry and pleasantly cool but at the same time abundantly sunny; and adequate money to permit a satisfactory diet is available to all. Most important, complete medical care is conveniently and cheaply available. Employees are encouraged to take advantage of the medical services, and the plantation nurse and doctor attend to many minor injuries and ailments for which persons in other communities might have recourse to home therapy. This willingness of the medical staff to treat even the most trivial injuries or pathologies serves importantly to safeguard the health of the community and also to discourage the use of the traditional magico-religious therapy of the Philippines and Japan.

The Territorial Department of Health is active in programs of health education and in providing free inoculation against communicable diseases. A program of instruction in the care of infants and children is well attended by mothers and expectant mothers of the community.

Plantation employment exposes the workers to no special types of industrial injuries or diseases, and it leaves ample time for rest, sleep, and recreation. The plantation maintains a very active safety program, and the labor union also is vigilant in these matters. Protective goggles have been mandatory for decades for employees working among pineapple plants, the sharp leaves of which may cause serious injuries to the eyes. The single type of industrial accident which occurs rather frequently is "pine pokes"—punctures, usually slight, in the region of the face by the stiff, needlelike points of pineapple leaves. Every fore-seeable hazard is met with precautionary devices, and serious accidents are uncommon.

Life for most residents of Maunaloa is highly secular. Religion does not seem to enter importantly into community affairs or daily living. Regular services are conducted in the small wooden Catholic chapel, which stands out sharply from all other buildings by virtue of its coat of vivid blue-green paint. Services for a few other religious faiths (in 1956 only Mormon and Full Gospel Mission) may be held intermittently in community clubhouses or private homes. Adherents of other faiths may attend services in outside communities on the island, but few appear to do so. Only Catholicism, the faith of nearly all Filipino residents, is well represented. Most Japanese are nominal Buddhists, but religion seems important to most of them only when a relative or a friend dies. Weekly participation in temple rites is not a feature of Japanese Buddhism, although traditional rites are held at irregular times throughout the year. The lone Buddhist temple is located seventeen miles away, in the town of Kaunakakai, and attendance by Maunaloa Japanese is poor.

The dominant attitude toward religion appears to be indifferent acceptance. Actual church attendance as against ideal attendance or opportunities for attendance is very small even among Catholics, who may attend church with little effort. Missionaries have been active for decades, but they have made little impression on the people. Despite a vigorous Baptist campaign which included, in 1956, an attractive and fairly well attended summer program for children—a kindergarten-like Bible school of three weeks followed by two weeks of summer camp at the seaside, with food and lodging provided for a nominal fee—no conversions were made. Expressed reasons of some parents for enrolling their children in this church program were that well-chaperoned recreation away from home was good for the children and it gave their mothers a welcome rest.

As in other communities of Hawaii, young Mormon elders are familiar visitors. Despite decades of proselyting and the fact that the church is well represented on the island among the Hawaiian and part-Hawaiian populations, few conversions have been made at Maunaloa. Most of the less-than-a-dozen adult Mormons of the community brought their faith with them. The church custom of tithing and injunctions against smoking and drinking hold little appeal for other residents.

Only 28 per cent (134 of 474 on whom these statistics were based) of plantation employees are American citizens. Nearly all aliens are Philippine nationals, a substantial number of whom might easily qualify for American citizenship if they went through the formalities of naturalization. The only other alien employees are ten aged Japanese and one recently arrived European. The twenty Philippine-born employees who have become naturalized American citizens constitute the most socially and occupationally prominent men of the Filipino group. *Lunas* are almost invariably naturalized citizens. American citizenship is virtually unattainable by some Filipinos because they are illiterate and know little spoken English. Many have vague intentions of returning to the Philippines, perhaps when they retire on pension at the age of sixty-five. Some express a desire to return to their native land for a visit of inspection, at which time they will decide whether to remain or return to Hawaii. Others dream of using the savings they might acquire in Hawaii to purchase land in the Philippines for a song and then living out their lives in luxury there as socially important rich men. Few are consistently thrifty, however, and the dreams of most will remain dreams.

Many Filipinos appear to be indifferent about gaining citizenship. To do so would require burdensome study and examination, tasks which are easy to defer. Most important, American citizenship would convey no immediate advantage and would alter the daily course of their lives in almost no respect.

It is both difficult and unsatisfactory to generalize about the peoples of the community. Differences in attitude and custom associated with country of birth and with occupational assignment in Hawaii are too great. Forming a community which is "unnatural" in the sense that a common source of livelihood represents the only force which originally brought them together, the peoples who comprise the town of Maunaloa remain culturally as well as socially distinct and are most easily described separately.

IV | *The Filipinos*

Coming from twenty different and sometimes widely separated provinces of the Philippines, the Filipinos of the community are diverse in culture as well as speech. Four linguistic groups are important: Ilocano, Visayan, Pangasinan, and Tagalog. Native speakers of Ilocano, principally from the provinces of Ilocos Norte and Ilocos Sur, comprise nearly 70 per cent of the total Philippine-born population of approximately 350 people. Persons from Pangasinan and the Visayan Islands represent approximately 10 per cent each, and "Tagalogs," those who speak Tagalog as their first language, total about 5 per cent. A sprinkling of men and women are of other Philippine provenience, sometimes lone representatives of a province.

As might be inferred from these statistics, Ilocano culture dominates. Ilocanos and Tagalogs are usually the most closely associated of the four groups, and Visayans hold themselves aloof from other Filipino groups to the greatest degree. Although there are only thirty-five Visayans, they wield a disproportionate influence in community affairs. Earlier arrivals in Hawaii than the main body of Ilocanos, and displacing the Tagalogs who had arrived still earlier, the Visayans are well established at Maunaloa. Tagalogs are now few in number, but their language is socially important.

Knowledge of the Tagalog language and the common bond of being Filipinos in a scene dominated by peoples of other racial and cultural backgrounds tend to pull the Filipinos together. Presenting a common front in mild opposition to the rest of the community, the Filipinos are still only poorly united within their own ranks. Many factors contribute to the lack of social cohesion: diversity of language and culture, differences in education and marital status, and differentials in occupational ranking and associated social prestige. Personal jealousies and dislikes hold apart even those within a common linguistic and cultural subgroup.

Many stereotypes formulated in the Philippines have been transplanted to Maunaloa. Any Filipino may say, for example, that the people of Batanes, the remote group of small islands stretching northwest of Luzon, are strange and incomprehensible because they "talk just like birds," although few can actually have heard Batanes speech either in the Philippines or from the lone native of Batanes in plantation employ. Filipinos of one subcultural affiliation often express, toward other peoples of their own nation, attitudes that appear to be the precise counterpart of those existing interculturally throughout the world: "those people" are never human in quite the same desirable sense in which the speakers are human. This attitude, although not necessarily invidious or antagonistic, tends to preserve social distances.

Invidious stereotypes and consistent if mild antagonism are, however, readily observable between the Ilocanos and the Visayans. Viewing themselves as quiet, refined, ethically superior people who are interested in music and the finer things of life, Visayans have a poor opinion of Ilocanos, whom they describe as crude, loudmouthed braggarts who drink and gamble too much, neglect the proper training of their children, and hold vulgarly elaborate christening rites, with godparents by the dozen rather than a single pair. Ilocanos, they say, eat dogs—and any Visayans at Maunaloa who eat dogs have learned to do so from Ilocanos. Ilocanos, in turn, call Visayans lazy, unreliable good-for-nothings. Visayans, they remark jokingly, are not "real Filipinos" because their skins are too light in color.

Although usually expressed in jesting tones, these stereotypes are indicative of the partial estrangement of Visayans and Ilocanos. Avoiding intimacy with Ilocanos, Visayans much prefer the company of other Visayans and marriage to other Visayans. Visayan and Ilocano raisers of fighting cocks tend to pit their birds against each other in bouts, which are ordinarily public, and to lay bets against each other.

The composition and activities of organized groups among Maunaloa Filipinos illustrate the lack of unity. All Maunaloa Filipinos and their dependents theoretically belong to the Kayumangi (Filipino) Club, which may sponsor dances for adults and provide refreshments and entertainment for children on the Fourth of July and Rizal Day, the great Philippine holiday which commemorates the death, on December

30, 1895, of the patriot José Rizal. The Kayumangi Club has shown only spasmodic activity and is not an important organization in either Filipino or community affairs. The Filipino Catholic Club, which concerns itself with care of the chapel, has a membership of less than forty persons. Most Filipinos evince little active interest in this or other community affairs; the Catholic Club is composed mainly of the small body of civic-minded Filipinos who have high prestige as social leaders. The Ladies' Altar Society, responsible for maintenance and care of the interior of the Catholic chapel, is open to any adult female member of the church. The twenty-five women who belong are among the civic-minded leaders in the Filipino community, the same persons who bear the load in other community affairs.

No truly active organization embraces all Filipinos of the community. The closest approaches are the Catholic Church and the local chapter of the labor union. Although predominantly Filipino in membership, they are not looked upon as Filipino in-groups.

Two small clubs theoretically restrict membership to Philippine cultural subgroups. These are mutual-aid societies, which charge entrance fees and monthly dues. The funds are used to help members or their families to meet unusual expenses incurred by funerals, protracted illness, and the marriage festivities of their children. The Pangasinan Club, reduced in 1957 to semiactive status by a shortage of funds resulting from over-expansion, is limited to employees from Pangasinan and their dependents. The somewhat larger (35 adult male members early in 1956) Visayan Hinabangay ("aid" or "coöperation") Club, founded in 1955, was organized with the intent of limiting membership to employees from the Visayan Islands. Both societies include wives of various Philippine subcultural affiliations and Hawaii-born wives of a variety of extractions. They have also come to include, "by request," some adult men who are not Pangasinans or Visayans.

When a Filipino dies, it is the custom for friends of the family to canvass the Filipino community for contributions. Non-Filipinos also may be solicited if the deceased was among the relatively few Filipinos of community-wide social prestige or acquaintance. One of the stated reasons for the founding of the Visayan club was to avoid this general solicitation.

Filipinos may also belong to Territorial-wide funeral associations, which advertise on the radio. These organizations commonly operate by charging a small entrance fee; and, because all funds collected are said to be paid to dependents upon the death of a member, all the members pay the fee again each time a death occurs.

Filipinos may be divided into two groups, based upon the time of their arrival in Hawaii. Those who arrived in Hawaii under labor contract in 1946 are distinctive in a number of respects from the earlier arrivals, nearly all of whom reached Hawaii before official importation of labor ceased in 1931. The eighty-three employees of the plantation, who comprise the 1946 arrivals, are nearly all Ilocanos and live in Maunaloa. Better educated than their older countrymen, they average nearly four years of formal schooling as opposed to less than two years. Few among them are illiterate and many are fairly proficient in English, expressing themselves in terms that combine flowery, old-fashioned words and phrases with very modern slang.

Principally men between thirty-five and forty years of age, the Filipinos of this group are considerably younger than other Philippine-born employees, and the percentage of married men among them is much greater. Sixty of the eighty-three are married, but many of this number left their wives and families in the Philippines because their original intent was to remain in Hawaii for only a few years. Most of these men still plan to return to their families at the indefinite time when they have saved "enough" money.

Better accquainted with American ways at the time of their arrival than most of their countrymen in the community, the 1946 group adjusted quickly to life in Hawaii. According to the statements of older Filipino employees, the new arrivals "taught us a lot." Plantation supervisors describe these men as a "little less easy to work with" than other Filipinos. An occasional supervisory employee describes them as tending to be "fresh" or "cocky." Other Filipinos may describe them in the same terms, explaining that these tendencies are "natural" because the younger Filipinos suffered much oppression during the Japanese occupation of the Philippines, when some of them served as members of guerrilla forces.

Despite differences in customs and attitudes, the 1946 arrivals do not constitute a socially distinct or united group. They have mixed well with their predecessors, most of whom also speak Ilocano. The only apparent social distance is from the Visayans, who, although maintaining peaceful relations with this group of countrymen as well as with others, hold themselves somewhat aloof.

Hawaii-born Filipino employees are young, few in number—only twelve are included among plantation personnel—and are usually sons or daughters of employees. Since many of them have grown up in the community, their relations with older Filipinos are excellent. They display affection and tolerance for their elders, and, in return, are regarded with fondness as well as with a measure of respect because of their superior education.

Despite excellent personal relations between the Hawaii-born and the immigrants, however, markedly different customs hold them amicably apart. The interests, ideals, and attitudes of the Hawaii-born follow familiar American patterns, given something of a Philippine cast. Their elders, although eagerly adopting certain American ways, cling to many of their native customs. Cockfighting and heavy gambling, for example, are the cherished pleasures of the Philippine-born males. The Hawaii-born Filipinos ordinarily gamble only in friendly social games with trifling stakes, and seldom appear at cockfights even as spectators. Gambling and cockfighting, they say, are not shunned as immoral pastimes but merely as uninteresting.

The role of the young Hawaii-born Filipinos (with the exception of a few immigrant wives, other Filipinos are all past youth) is difficult to evaluate. After childhood they seldom continue to be members of the community. Girls ordinarily marry while very young, after the completion of high school or while still high-school students. Frequently they marry outside the community. Boys enter the army or take employment in Honolulu or other communities. In recent years a few Hawaii-born Filipinos have entered college, but the number is small. Despite unanimous agreement by the parents consulted that college education is highly desirable, few of them regard a college education for their children as a goal which they are financially able to meet. Among some dozens of Filipino and part-Filipino children of Maunaloa who have matured within the last decade, informants could recall only five who had entered colleges or universities. Filipino youths from Maunaloa, however, tend increasingly to further their education in trade schools in Honolulu or on the mainland, and in recent years a few young Filipino women have taken nurse's training or other professional work.

Highly Americanized in customs and attitudes, the Hawaii-born Filipinos doubtless serve importantly during childhood in introducing American ways to their elders. As adults they are too few in number to constitute an important group in the community.

An additional circumstance which inhibits unity among the Filipinos is the very large number of men without spouses. Totaling 224 of the 306 permanent male Filipino residents in the summer of 1956, the effectively single stood in a ratio with their married fellows of approximately three to one. Of this group, nearly one-third had wives residing in the Philippines. Living at the lowermost edge of the settlement in partial isolation, the single men lead an existence marginal to that of the main pulse of community life. Most of them live in a masculine world which affords few social contacts with women except of the most casual sort.

Repressed sexual drives among these men appear to be the source of little manifest discord in the community. Loose women can cause serious trouble among both single and married men, and they have done so at various times in the history of the plantation. For the most part, however, the single men of today constitute a peaceful group among whom sexual drives seem to be well disciplined. Prostitutes have for years been prohibited from entering Maunaloa, and are rigidly excluded from other communities on the island by the police and the Department of Public Health. The island abounds with gossip about loose women, but it seems certain that no out-and-out prostitute has been able during the past decade to practice her profession in or near the community for more than a brief period.

Women are nevertheless in great demand and at a very great premium. Any unattached physically mature female may easily attract a large group of suitors, and a young and reasonably attractive girl is a virtual belle. Filipino residents themselves state that the community has a bad reputation with respect to sexual morality, and that the scarcity of women is the major contributing factor. They regard as the most serious examples of local immorality the several common-law unions in which the males are Filipinos.

Many older Filipino men and women compare Philippine standards of morality with those among Filipinos in Hawaii and in their community, stating that much behavior accepted and common in Hawaii is severely condemned in the Philippines. The divorce rate, they state, is exceptionally high among Hawaiian Filipinos; marital infidelity is common, and Hawaii-born Filipino girls of the community are almost invariably pregnant at the time of marriage. Truth and fiction or exaggeration are intermingled in these statements. Divorces are certainly not uncommon among Filipinos, but they seem to occur most frequently at Maunaloa when the marriages are between Filipino men and non-Filipino women. In the history of the community, Filipino girls have almost invariably been pregnant, and sometimes well along in pregnancy, at the time of the medical examination required to secure a marriage license.

The extent of extramarital sexual relations, however, is not so readily measurable. Gossip concerning illicit relations is plentiful, and doubtless is exaggerated. Illegitimate children are rare—if the offspring of a few long-established common-law marriages are excepted. Standards of sexual morality among Filipino residents are in fact quite varied. Perhaps the most useful comments are those of several Filipino men and women who made an informal analysis of the Filipino social groups of the community. Most Filipino members, they state, fit into one of three groups: the quiet and conservative (of middle and advanced middle age), the wild ones (usually but not always somewhat younger than the conservatives), and the young people (Hawaii-born and, as a group, seldom regarded as being wild).

Few Filipino women were classified by the informants as belonging to the "wild crowd." Most of the couples so described are Cosmopolitan unions of Filipino men and wives of non-Filipino extraction. Conservatives, however, exercise few if any social sanctions to make the nonconformists fall into line. Almost any member of the Filipino community, regardless of the blackness of his reputation with regard to sexual morality, appears to be accepted cordially by most if not all others, even though habitual association and intimacy may be avoided.

This attitude of tolerance is said to have applied also to male Filipinos who, in former times, secretly and illegally arranged to have prostitutes from Honolulu visit the community and served as pimps for them. These entrepreneurs are said to have suffered little if any social stigma among other Filipinos.

Filipino men state that the plantation policy of banning prostitutes was successful in part because of their own actions. Circumvention required discretion and secrecy. To avoid giving away the show, the employee-entrepreneur invited only a small clientele. Word got about among the single men very quickly, however, and ill feeling—it could hardly be called sexual jealousy—evoked by failure to receive an invitation is said to have prompted some men to inform the island police by telephone.

The tale is told that in years gone by, when feminine companionship was at a premium, one Filipino mother of the community turned her daughters to economic advantage. While acting as a strict chaperone, she would allow the most acceptable young Filipino men the privilege, at a fee of twenty-five cents each, of chatting with her daughters in the family living room.

A few of the single men have sweethearts on other islands, whom they visit on weekends. Some occasionally visit prostitutes on Maui or Oahu; and, according to gossip, a small number of single men have "arrangements" with married women of their own or other communities, but the number of such relationships is probably small.

A reflection of the premium placed upon femininity is the great success of *ripa* (raffles) conducted among the single men by women who visit the community near paydays intermittently throughout the year. Raffles are full-fledged parties, with a suggestion of naughtiness about them, rather than merely games of chance. *Ripa* women, who are of various genetic strains but all well versed in Philippine customs, come singly or in groups of two or three. They are eagerly welcomed by many single men, who make raffles into parties, and prepare elaborate food for them.

Raffles are held in the single men's houses. Usually there is music and dancing. Each man who has bought a ticket for an aloha shirt or some other raffle prize is entitled to dance with the woman conducting the raffle. Goods which are raffled are easily available on the island or by order from Honolulu. They bring disproportionately large sums of money to their female purveyors, but raffle tickets are important primarily as the price of admission to the desirable company of females whose chief stock in trade is sociability.

Much gossip revolves about the morality of the *ripa* women, but few if any of them seem to be prostitutes. The number who actually visit the camp is probably no more than a dozen a year, a figure much less than rumor would have it. Several wives of the community are said to have first reached Maunaloa when they came to conduct raffles.

The single men include an asexual group to whom intimate relations with women are, or have come to be, unnecessary. The fact that these men are of middle or advanced middle age undoubtedly has some bearing on the matter, but social selection seems a more important factor. Similar communities of asexual men—voluntary associations rather than forced groupings brought about by law or accident, such as soldiers or prisoners—have been noted in other parts of the world. It seems reasonable to think that the nature of plantation life at Maunaloa selects single men for whom the company of women is unnecessary or less necessary than for others. Throughout the years a process of sifting and segregation has evidently taken place, with the malcontents taking wives or finding positions in larger towns or the city of Honolulu, and the troublemakers suffering dismissal. The body of single men remaining on the plantation thus consists of persons to whom this manner of life is acceptable or even preferred.

The precise nature of relationships among these men who live in a masculine world is little known, even to the most knowledgeable and interested of plantation administrators. Without the aid of special and elaborate techniques of interviewing, the men themselves are unable to verbalize on this subject. Most relationships with other men are habitual relations, whatever these may be, and therefore escape verbalizing or special attention. The unusual in relationships, however, may be volubly and passionately voiced. The Filipino—single or married, male or female—who dislikes another may vent his hostility freely, heaping abuse and condemnation upon the object of his dislike.

In the first decade of the plantation's existence, arguments over women, gambling, and money often led to physical violence, occasionally to murder. But for some quarrels the stated or immediate cause seems too trivial to have had such serious consequences, and suggests the familiar pattern of mounting irritation and strain among men who are forced to live constantly in close association. The murder of a man by his roommate is said to have been the culmination of a dispute over whether their bedroom window should have been open or closed while they slept. A fight which resulted in minor physical injury began as an argument over the relative superiority of the flavor of black versus spotted pigs. Another incident involving blows but no injury is said to have arisen out of jealousy while flying kites, a form of amusement learned in the Philippines. One man's kite flew higher than the other.

Filipinos themselves say that jealousy is a primary cause of strained relations, which, although serious, may never develop into outright quarrels. The man who pushes upward, who attains a position of relatively high income or who acquires desirable possessions, gains prestige thereby, but at the same time he arouses the envy of his less fortunate companions.

A single man ordinarily shares a house with several other single men. His bedroom, which he locks in his absence to prevent theft, contains most of his possessions: bedding, clothing, frequently a radio, and a variety of small objects including photographs of relatives.

The men share a living room, kitchen, and toilet and laundry facilities. The small living room, dark because of its central location in the house flanked by bedrooms, is furnished with a rough wooden table, benches, and a few straight chairs. Single men seldom own a television set because it is expensive and, unless everyone owns a set, is likely to become a bone of contention. The facts that single men are little versed in English and the group least Americanized in customs also discourage ownership of television sets.

The kitchen contains a refrigerator, shared by all, and a number of ovenless kerosene stoves. Most men individually own not only stoves but also cooking utensils and tableware. Close friends may share this equipment and jointly prepare their meals. Most men like to have the company of others even while cooking separately and preparing their own food. Coöperation in performing household tasks is worked out over longer periods of association, and discord among housemates is uncommon. A man can, in any case, change houses if tensions develop.

A few men eat frequently at the community restaurant, which serves principally American dishes and boiled rice, but most single men do their own marketing and preparation of food, including lunches to be eaten in the fields on workdays.

Standards of cleanliness in single men's quarters, although lower than among families, are fairly high. Some of the men retain the Philippine custom of cutting a hole in the floor into which dust and other small refuse is swept so that it falls on the ground two or three feet beneath the floor. In former times, before detached communal latrines serving many dwellings were replaced by modern toilets in homes, this practice was a source of concern to plantation authorities over sanitary conditions because these apertures might be used as urinals at night.

In the course of a year a single man has much free time. Besides the hundred-odd days normally free of work, additional time averaging nearly twenty days is taken on individual initiative. Officially sanctioned as sick leave, these days are frequently taken simply to rest, to indulge in recreation, or to visit friends elsewhere.

Most important of the free-time interests of single men, as well as many of the married Filipinos, are cockfighting and gambling. The rearing and training of fighting cocks are elaborate, expensive, and time-consuming activities which are pursued with intense devotion. Much of one's income may be poured into the keeping of gamecocks and the associated gambling. Feed for the birds, all of which must be purchased, is expensive, and the birds themselves are costly, ranging in price from $25 to $30 for ordinary mature males to several hundred dollars or more for birds of high repute. Until importation to Hawaii by ship was forbidden in the summer of 1956, birds were obtained from breeders in the continental United States, and they are also hatched and raised in the community. An enthusiast might own as many as thirty mature cocks and give most of his free time to their care and training.

Fights are held nearly every Sunday from the end of December to August, when the fowls begin to molt. From August to Christmas, when cocks are in poor feather, few bouts are held. The locale alternates between Maunaloa and Kualapuu, the community associated with a pineapple plantation about fifteen miles from Maunaloa. Convenient open spaces within or at the margins of the two communities are the cockfighting arenas.

Birds are carefully matched for size and weight before the bouts begin. This process may require lengthy discussion as well as the customary feeling of the bodies of the fowl to estimate their weight and relative musculature. Beliefs tinged with supernaturalism exist about the supremacy of white cocks, which some men refer to as "kings of the chickens, with more power," and owners of the far more common colored birds may be reluctant to match them with white fowl. But the white nevertheless find matches, which they win no more frequently than the colored cocks.

From the standpoint of the welfare of the birds, cockfighting as practiced at Maunaloa is not sport but lethal encounter which almost invariably results in the death of one cock, and the death of both contestants is not uncommon. The birds rarely give up until they are physically incapable of continuing to fight. Gaffs are never used. Molokai cockfights are stronger fare. The weapons attached to the cock's legs are wicked five-inch slasher blades, thin crescents of steel honed to razor sharpness, which can virtually disembowel as well as kill by piercing.

Slasher blades often reach vital organs quickly, and bouts, seldom enduring more than a few minutes, may end with the death of one bird within thirty seconds. Only the fact that fighting cocks are small animals with little blood saves the bouts from being very gory spectacles. The spectators show little obvious excitement, however, unless the birds are exceptional performers. The unusually brave cock may elicit shouts of encouragement, and the very rare bird which exhibits cowardice evokes a much greater verbal response in derision.

Fights get off to a slow start about seven o'clock in the morning, but few bouts are fought until after nine o'clock. It is hard for a stranger to tell when a bout will begin. Men cluster in small groups about the arena. Tethered in the shade of buildings and trees are the fighting cocks, surprisingly docile creatures until they have been pitted against other birds. The largest knot of men stands and squats at the arena proper, a flat area of exposed red earth. No audible signal announces that a match is about to begin. Owners of birds emerge from beneath trees or from the yards of nearby houses, carrying the cocks, with slasher blades and protective sheaths affixed, to the arena. Even the sleepiest and most disinterested-looking spectators become aware of the event about to occur. In a few moments a hundred or more individuals may assemble about the cocks, their owners, and the referee. Bets are placed between individuals as the owners and trainers go through the elaborate preliminaries, stroking the cocks, blowing on them, and holding the two birds together so that they peck at each other's heads and become enraged. Sheaths are removed and the cocks are finally released at a signal from the referee. After a few moments of violence the issue is settled. When the referee has declared the winner, bets are paid, the winner takes his bird and the dead cock of his opponent, and the spectators disperse. A foraging dog or two, attracted by the smell of blood, sniffs the blood-soaked dust, licks experimentally, and drifts away.

At increasingly short intervals the whole procedure recurs, until finally, at the height of activity just before noon, bouts follow one another with such rapidity that spectators do not leave the arena. After an interval for lunch, matches continue until mid-afternoon.

Most of the spectators and bet-layers at the cockfights are males. Cockfights are considered inappropriate events for children, and they are seldom present. The few women in attendance are a mixed group of Filipinos and Cosmopolitans. Most women consider the bouts unpleasantly brutal, and the well-bred Filipino woman does not attend. Many wives and children of male participants in the cockfights may, however, be in the vicinity. Accompanying their husbands and fathers from Kualapuu to Maunaloa, or the reverse, they visit friends in the host community or remain in their cars. A few older women may set up temporary shops near the arena to sell Filipino and American foods and soft drinks. Alcoholic beverages are seldom in evidence. Cockfights are not an occasion for dress-up clothing or for drunkenness, although some may get drunk when the fights have ended.

An even greater attraction than the cockfights are various forms of table gambling which bear no relation to the fights but are conducted nearby at the same time. The combined participants in cockfighting and gambling may total several hundred people. Rows of wooden tables are set up in convenient shady spots, with a man operating each table. These entrepreneurs are mostly employees of the two plantations, but they include other residents of Molokai and professional gamblers. A participant may take his choice of craps or a cosmopolitan variety of card games, including games of Chinese, Spanish, or Philippine origin. Fashions in games vary. Among the most popular in 1956 were *paikyao*, *haikyu* (both Chinese), *payut* (Filipino), rummy, and poker. The stranger to Filipino customs must learn quickly that he cannot touch a Filipino friend engaged in gambling. To do so would arouse antagonism, because the practice is believed to result in bad luck.

Participants in these games of chance generally include a greater number of non-Filipinos and a few more women than do the cockfights, and larger sums of money are involved. After one of the heavy paydays of the summer season, several thousands of dollars change hands at these gambling sessions.

Both cockfighting and gambling are illegal in the Territory of Hawaii, but Molokai is in some ways off the beaten track of conventional Hawaiian norms. These pastimes are the joy of many people. They do not ordinarily interfere with work and today do not often result in quarrels. Officials of both plantations continue their old policy of ignoring these practices, and the small police force takes only token measures to prevent them. With the exception of gambling, cockfighting, and, to a lesser degree, poaching on private lands, Molokai residents are generally law-abiding. A police force large enough to control gambling on Molokai and a jail capable of holding even a fraction of the inveterate gamblers are economic impossibilities. Island police raid the cockfights and the gambling tables frequently, but make few arrests. Fighting cocks and gambling devices can easily be carried away or concealed; bouts do not last long and can be put to an end quickly, and policemen are highly visible. It is said that the owner of a fighting cock cannot be arrested unless the bird is wearing slasher blades or is actually fighting. Customarily the police make arrests only when they can lay hands on the owners of two pitted birds, but the culprits are fleet of foot and can dodge elusively in and out of the houses nearby. Catching table gamblers in the act is even more difficult.

After a raid all illegal activities cease until the police leave the community. Interrupted pastimes are resumed after the few moments needed for preparation, and the scene may shift to another area. The standard fine for cockfighting is $25, hardly a deterrent to an avid cock fancier. Filipinos say that the first arrest is annoying because it requires about three hours of detention at the police station in Kaunakakai for fingerprinting and other official procedures, most of which need not be repeated for subsequent arrests.

A popular pastime of both single and married men is playing pool, which may or may not involve gambling. Younger men play baseball, basketball, and volleyball on teams which compete with those of other communities.

Fishing is an important recreation among single men, who have lesser demands on their time. Line fishing, skin diving, torch fishing at night, spear fishing, and netting with small throw nets and stationary gill nets are all popular, and the single area of ocean beach readily and legally available for fishing is heavily worked. The Filipino fisherman may exceed the cock fancier in dedication. Men without automobiles walk a round trip of ten or more miles to the fishing grounds. The fisherman in his free hours may expend far more energy than during a working day, staying up most of the night until he catches some fish or is forced by lack of time to abandon the project. To return empty-handed is to admit serious failure.

Poaching of game and fish is said to be popular. All ocean frontage of western Molokai is privately owned, and plantation personnel are allowed free use of a relatively small strip about two miles long. Members of the community fishing club have the privilege of fishing in other and more desirable areas. But trespassing to fish in relatively little-used waters is attractive and not easily detected. Game laws with respect to size of fish and size and nature of nets may be broken easily without detection. Trespassing on private land to shoot introduced game birds or the small spotted Indian deer which live in the algarroba groves close to the sea is, however, a much more risky pursuit. Permission to hunt in these lands may be gained by payment of a fee, but few persons follow this procedure. Despite vigilance by landowners and the police, successful poaching is said to occur regularly. The practice is the subject of much conversation, and gossip probably greatly enlarges its incidence over the actual rate. The illicit shooting of a few deer during the year is sufficient to maintain tales of its prevalence. Filipinos are not the only malefactors involved. The two groups which are exempt from this charge are plantation Haoles and Japanese. Haoles have little reason to trespass; the few who desire to hunt may secure permission to enter private lands occasionally, with or without payment of a fee. Japanese are extraordinarily law-abiding.

A practice which is restricted to Filipinos and principally to single men among them is the holding of parties at which dogs are cooked and eaten. Like the poaching of deer, these events are not common, but they are the subject of much gossip. Regular participants estimate that from half a dozen to a dozen such parties may be held throughout the year. The feasts may be planned some days in advance, but are more likely to be impromptu, arranged while the men are under the influence of wine. Whether planned or not, the feasts are drunken affairs.

Dogs are sometimes purchased and—it is said—often stolen. They should be fat (most Maunaloa dogs appear well fed if not fat, whereas cats are commonly thin), short-haired, and darkly pigmented, preferably black. It seems that white dogs are never used because they taste bad or because of vaguely remembered taboos against eating them. After the hair has been singed and scraped off, the animal is eviscerated and the viscera cleaned for future consumption. Various recipes, differing according to the organ being prepared and the preference and state of drunkenness of the cook, involve boiling, frying, simmering, broiling, or only partial cooking. All the soft parts of the animal including the brains are eaten, and the blood is also consumed, sometimes while raw and warm. The practice of force-feeding dogs or goats with rice before slaughtering them so that they become, as it were, ready-stuffed is known to some of the older men, but it is said no longer to be observed.

Dog feasts take place outside, where open fires or portable Japanese charcoal braziers are used for cooking. The favorite place is the ocean beach, where participants may drink and act with little inhibition. As many as fifteen men may participate. Women are rarely present.

Filipinos are much condemned for this practice by other peoples of the community, some of whom lump in their condemnation all Filipinos for the behavior of the few. The prevailing attitude among Filipinos is that this practice is revolting if not immoral. Dog-eaters are well aware of this sentiment and seem in a curious way to share it, speaking of the dog feast in a defensively laughing tone as if it were a form of delinquency.

Tales about dog-eating abound. A Visayan woman tells the tragic love story of two dogs. After the woman's dog, a bitch, had been stolen and devoured at a dog feast, its devoted mate refused food, friendship, or consolation of any kind. Stricken by sorrow at his loss, he committed suicide three days later by lying down in the path of an oncoming automobile.

The eating of dog flesh is said to be the subject of practical jokes whereby persons who are violently opposed to the very thought of such a thing are tricked into partaking. Many stories of such deception circulate, although few of them can be verified. A common motif of these tales is that the victim is informed of his unwitting act by the barking of the pranksters just after he has swallowed the delicacy. A Filipino gang foreman who maintains very friendly relations with the men working under him states that the thought of such trickery has made him go without lunch in the field for fear that the practice of sharing food will be deliberately used to trick him for the amusement of the crew. Opportunities to perpetrate chicanery of this sort are in fact uncommon.

Convivial drinking is an important form of recreation for many single Filipino men as well as for some of the family men and their wives. Far outranking other alcoholic beverages in quantity purchased and consumed is a cheap California sherry sold in half-gallon and gallon jugs. A California tokay wine of similar quality runs a poor second in popularity. Camping spots beneath the algarroba trees at the employees' beach are littered with empty jugs, although most drinking is done within the confines of the camp. Beer, whisky, and mixed drinks are favored by the more Americanized of the Filipinos and by those of elevated social position. When money is scarce, especially during the slack winter months, some men make a home brew, the chief ingredient of which is brown sugar. If the brewer is not too impatient, a heady drink is obtained in two or three weeks.

An old custom, now long abandoned, was to make an alcoholic beverage of living pineapples directly in the field. A nearly ripe pineapple, still attached to the plant, served as both the chief ingredient and the brewer's vat. The formula consisted of severing the top with a knife to form a lid, cutting up the now exposed fruit into small pieces without puncturing the tough outer skin, adding sugar to the diced flesh, and replacing the top. After some days, the fruit was picked and its pulpy contents were strained through a cloth to eliminate the solid pineapple flesh as well as the small black beetles and fruit flies which swarm about overripe and damaged fruit. Employees who remember this practice are unanimous in appraising the finished product as mildly alcoholic but having a horrible taste.

Although consumption of liquor is great, especially among single men, alcoholics are rare. Some Filipinos are teetotalers, and most of the others drink to excess only on special occasions. In any case, alcoholism and plantation employment are incompatible. Chronically heavy drinkers cannot work with the regularity and the manual precision required. A menace to the safety of other employees as well as a poor economic investment to the corporation, they are eventually discharged if they do not mend their ways.

Music is a favorite form of recreation among Filipinos. The community boasts two amateur Filipino orchestras, and other Filipinos or part Filipinos play with outside orchestras. Dancing is a common accompaniment of wedding feasts and other Filipino parties. The more avid fanciers of music and dancing may also attend parties in other communities. In Kaunakakai two "night clubs" offer food, dancing, and sometimes floor shows by fourth-rate professional entertainers from Honolulu or the mainland. These gathering places are, however, patronized chiefly by non-Haoles from other communities of the island, and few of the residents of Maunaloa are among their habituees.

A popular amusement among Philippine-born residents is the weekly showing in the local theater of Filipino movies, played in the Tagalog language, which may last as long as three hours. Members of the audience may comment loudly on the activities portrayed, to the amusement of others and the self-credit of themselves as wits. Attendance is frequently a family affair enjoyed by the children. Young Hawaii-born adults attend less often. American movies, shown on three additional nights of the week, are not popular. Usually old and third-rate, they cannot compete with home television.

Excepting the card game *payut*, Philippine games and diversions are uncommon. The Philippine kick-ball game called *sipa* has not been seen for many years. Men occasionally make and fly kites, but most diversions are of Western origin, whether learned in Hawaii or the Philippines.

The most common and important form of entertainment for Filipino families is watching television. Almost all Filipino families own sets, as do most other families of the community. Reception from Honolulu is excellent, and television—much more popular than radio has ever been in the community—has unquestionably done much to bring the residents of Maunaloa into closer contact with the rest of the nation.

The life of the Filipino woman is one of many privileges. Holding a high status with relationship to males at home in the Philippines, her position is enhanced in Hawaii, where she is a scarce commodity. Filipino women make these statements about themselves and add, with what appears to be a measure of truth, that they do not take advantage of their husbands as do some of the non-Filipino women married to Filipino men. Some of these women, they say, spend all their husbands' money, and expect the husbands to cook and wash for the family as well as work in the fields.

Filipino wives are housekeepers and mothers, but they are not drudges who subordinate themselves entirely to the wants and welfare of the family. Generally self-assured, secure women, they have a voice in family affairs, and take time for recreation. Their status with respect to males is indicated by the telephone listings. A substantial number of telephones in Filipino families are listed under the wife's name (e.g.,

Mrs. Estrelita Lopez), a practice rarely found among other peoples of the community.

Perhaps the most important pastime for Filipino women is chatting with other women. Although few Filipino women indulge in gambling at the cockfights, many play cards in their homes with other women, and some are inveterate home gamblers. By curious transposition, one of the most popular forms of gambling is the Japanese *sakura* (cherry), a game played with imported Japanese cards bearing no writing but only flowers and other ornamental pictures. Once played by Japanese males in the community, *sakura* is now almost entirely the game of Filipino women and women of other ethnic groups who are the wives of Filipino men.

The attitudes and practices of the women of the Filipino community show wide variations. Old women may preserve many Philippine customs. Mutual tolerance and affection mark the relationships between the Hawaii-born women and girls and their Philippine-born mothers. A Hawaii-born girl would never, even in old age, follow the older women's Philippine custom of smoking cigarettes "backward" (that is, with the lighted end in the mouth), but she does not deride the practice among her elders. The old sometimes disparage or express bewilderment at the attitudes and habits of the young, but relations are nevertheless warm and tolerant.

It is considered appropriate and desirable for unmarried girls to dress well, look attractive, and enjoy the approved pleasures of life. Well before she has turned eighteen, the Filipino girl has usually become a trim and attractive young lady who devotes much time and thought to clothing, hairdress, and makeup and is a graceful ballroom dancer. Secure in the knowledge that she is the object of masculine admiration, she is usually poised in social relationships.

Nearly all Filipinos are members of the Catholic Church, and many regard themselves as devout. Services, however, are poorly attended, especially by men. The chapel, with a seating capacity of ninety-odd persons, is said to be filled on some occasions, but few men are present. Judging from events during 1956, a baptism or wedding attracts only a small number of persons to the chapel for the ritual itself, but many attend the secular feast and entertainment which follow. All the conventional Catholic ceremonies marking the critical events of life are observed. Almost everyone is baptized, confirmed, married, and interred with church rites, performed by a European priest who serves at more than one chapel on the island. Children receive conventional instruction in dogma. But religion does not appear to weigh heavily on Filipinos. The facts that the Filipinos do not form a well-knit unit and that many Filipino men have non-Filipino and non-Catholic wives may be noted as influences inhibiting church attendance.

A very few Filipinos are members of the Church of Jesus Christ of Latter-Day Saints (Mormon), and a dozen men and women, including several non-Filipino wives of Filipino men, in recent years have joined a small evangelical sect which meets in the homes of members. The noisy procedures of their prayer meetings are described by other Filipinos as strange and puzzling.

Twelve men and women are members of the Filipino Federation of America, a quasi-religious organization with manifold aims and aspects, which include the establishment of American-Philippine rapport and the self-improvement of its members through adherence to religious-moral precepts. Maunaloa Filipinos who are Federation members do not gamble or drink, and are opposed to "vices" of all kinds. They like to play golf, an activity approved by Hilario Moncado, the recently deceased founder and leader of the organization. They characteristically avoid membership in the labor union on the grounds that their leader disapproved of strikes. Federation members may belong to the Catholic Church, although some express confusion on this point. If—they say—they were "spiritual" members of the Federation rather than "material" or "liberal" members, they would devote themselves to religious study of a prescribed and non-Catholic kind. "Spiritual" members, fairly common in the community before World War II, followed strict dietary regulations and did not cut their hair but wore it braided under knitted caps. According to a well-circulated tale, they avoided all foods of animal origin except Carnation milk, which was unobjectionable because it comes from a flower. Whether or not this belief may once have been held, Carnation milk is certainly among the foods favored by all Federation members.

Supernaturalistic beliefs and practices of persons born in the Philippines are not pure Catholicism but a composite which includes elements of aboriginal Philippine religions, Spanish folk beliefs, and a scattering of customs of other origin. Faith in ghosts, sorcerers, and supernatural monsters is confined to the older and least well educated, and is on the

wane. Young people view these ideas as somewhat amusing superstitions. Even skeptics, however, may relate delicious, spine-tingling tales
of ghosts and ominous stories of malevolent sorcerers.

Native Filipino, Hawaiian, Japanese, Spanish, and other European
ghosts and monsters are all incorporated in the fearsome or mysterious
roster. Filipino ghosts, identified as *aswang* in Visayan, haunt every
tree. Sometimes they are young women or girls, sometimes—with a
presumably Spanish origin—ghostly horsemen or horsewomen accompanied by dogs. Some persons have at midnight seen the specter of a
young Haole woman who inhabits the small banyan tree before the post
office. *Obake*, Japanese monsters, are at least talked about, and Hawaiian *menehune* are said to haunt fishing areas along the beach. A
"*menehune* line," the customary path of travel of the little people of
Hawaii who are active only at night, passes through one of the dwellings
on The Hill.

Talk circulates also about *kahunas*, a word of Hawaiian derivation
meaning "priest," but which in this context always means sorcerer or
diviner. Given the right informants, one may gather many tales of successful image magic and of divination. Such tales abound also in other
communities of Molokai, especially among Hawaiians and part Hawaiians. Traditionally the Hawaiian center of sorcery and in ancient
times the home of the most powerful sorcerers, Molokai has preserved
many of its tales. Sorcery has probably never been practiced at Maunaloa, but it is the subject of idle talk among some of the older people.
In Kaunakakai it was important enough—probably only as a topic of
conversation—to have warranted a sermon by the Catholic priest in the
summer of 1956 inveighing against this belief. Tales about sorcery
seem seldom to charge Filipinos with the performance of black or harmful magic. The accounts, often vague and handed down many times,
usually attribute these acts to Hawaiians or, less frequently, to Portuguese.

Some Philippine supernaturalistic practices are still followed. A man
who weaves a fish net makes an offering to the spirits by pouring a little
wine on the net before using it. A Philippine-born man who purchases
a fishing boat usually holds a launching party and offers wine to the
spirits. A wine bottle must not be capped until all drinking has ceased,
and one's cup must not be turned upside down over the wine container.
Hair in a mole on a masculine face should not be plucked (many older

men pluck rather than shave their scanty beards). To violate these prohibitions would result in bad luck. At baptismal and wedding feasts and other large parties, a little of each of the principal banquet foods is placed in a special dish as an offering to the spirits. Old Filipinos may still follow the traditional practice of killing a white chicken and inspecting its entrails to determine the future or the auspiciousness of some important course of action. If the objective of divination is the diagnosis of illness, discolored organs of the dead fowl indicate the seat of the human ailment.

Young Filipinos raised in the community remember many practices followed by their parents which have almost disappeared within the last decade. To protect an infant from malevolent spirits which might injure him or cause death by stealing his soul, the parents would place garlic, ginger root, or sprinklings of salt around windows and doors at night or attach the two herbs to a string and tie it around the child's neck. Similar practices served to keep away the fearsome quakquak bird, which is especially attracted to new mothers and infants. Evil spirits might be exorcised or barred from a dwelling by braiding rags and burning them and by sprinkling salt and rice about the house. Food cooked for an ailing neighbor might be protected from evil influence during delivery by sprinkling the cover of the container with salt.

Many beliefs associating good and bad luck with household procedures formerly existed, but they have nearly disappeared except among the aged. These beliefs included injunctions against sweeping at night, allowing the rice measure to be empty, and sweeping up dry rice accidentally dropped on the floor—it must instead be picked up grain by grain with the fingers.

Practices of sympathetic and contagious magic remembered by older Filipinos, but considered ridiculous by the young, range from love magic to formulas for curing disease. Securing a hair from the head of a girl to the tail of a bird and releasing the bird will cause the girl's mind to get "tangled" so that she falls in love with the magician. Inserting a needle into the ground where a girl has urinated (an action generally impossible as well as absurd in Hawaii) will produce the same effect.

Supernaturalistic practices associated with the curing of illness are still sometimes observed. Certain of these represent curious and complementing blends of Christianity and native Philippine beliefs. Older

Filipinos sometimes make or obtain from others Good Friday oil (coconut oil made on Good Friday), which has special power for healing cuts and bruises and soothing pain. When a family moves into a house, it is customary to ask the Catholic priest to bless it by sprinkling consecrated water, thereby at the same time—from the point of view of the occupants—exorcising evil spirits. The old Philippine idea that death results from loss or theft of the soul is also compatible with Catholicism. "What can doctors and medicine do," one Filipino woman explained, "when the soul is gone?"

A few individuals, principally children, who have experienced a series of misfortunes or protracted illnesses, have had their given names changed to bring about a turn for the better in their fortunes. (This custom is followed in rural Japan also, but no evidence was found of its practice among Maunaloa Japanese.)

Name-changing for other reasons has been very common among male Filipinos of the community. Many men arrived in Hawaii under the names of other persons, taking these aliases because they were under age or because they were serving as substitutes for men who had signed labor contracts. Assumed names also allowed them to escape obligations and penalties for misdeeds in both the Philippines and Hawaii. Personnel records of the plantation contain many entries presumably correcting aliases to the true names. Correction has generally been made at the instigation of the men themselves, who must provide reasonable proof of age and place of birth under the corporation pension plan and for matters connected with passports and entry into Hawaii of dependents.

Magic associated with birth was fairly common until recent years. Pregnant women were under many half-believed taboos of diet and behavior to avoid misfortune. These injunctions included prohibitions against eating seaweed lest the fingers of the child be withered, and against playing with dolls lest the child be witless and doll-like. More important and common were practices concerned with the placenta and umbilical cord. Custom required the father of a newborn child to secure the placenta and bury it. After the infant's umbilical cord had dropped off, it was retained for future use in curing illness, and was traditionally kept in a bamboo tube beneath the raised floor of the house. Therapy consisted of grinding up part of the invalid's umbilical cord and having him swallow it.

The custom of burying the placenta (followed in similar manner by Japan-born Japanese) declined sharply after 1950, when the Maunaloa hospital closed and bed patients were transported to a hospital in a nearby community. Nurses of the present hospital report that patients rarely request the placenta. Philippine-born orderlies at the Maunaloa hospital had automatically delivered it to Filipino and Japanese fathers and thus helped preserve the practice of burial. To receive the placenta today, one must request it—and thereby make the embarrassing admission that he follows a barbaric foreign custom.

Despite the foregoing catalogue of surviving magical practices, the theory of disease and the medical procedures followed by the Filipinos are generally modern. When one is sick he consults a doctor. The traditional cures embodying supernaturalism are used only by some of the aged, and complement rather than replace diagnosis and treatment by a trained physician.

Folk practices of medicine among their patients seldom come to the attention of community physicians. For fear of almost certain disapproval, these activities are concealed from the doctor. Filipinos of Maunaloa are much less likely to hide the use of magical therapy from the plantation nurse, however, because she is socially less distant. Having served them sympathetically for many years, she is regarded as an understanding friend and helper. Her observations, agreeing with those of Filipino informants, are that magical cures hold little importance and are disappearing. During fifteen years of service she has heard patients talk about magic formulas of cure but has directly observed their use only rarely. The incident she recalls most vividly occurred in 1947, and such magical significance as it might have had was unknown to her. On the ground that it was harmless, the doctor then permitted friends and relatives of a Filipino dying of heart failure to administer a traditional Philippine cure. Ginger root, leaves, and other unidentified substances were wrapped in a banana leaf and covered with a cloth. Seven of these poultices were applied to the patient, two each of equal size to the ankles, knees, and arms, and the seventh and larger was laid over "the ball," as they called the heart. The patient died, but the cure was thought to have been of some therapeutic value to its administrators.

According to members of the Molokai office of the Territorial Department of Public Health, the use of folk remedies and magical cures is less common among Hawaiian plantation employees than among people of the lower economic and social classes of the city of Honolulu. (See "Inter-Island Nurses Bulletin," *Hawaii Medical Journal*, 1955 and 1956, for a series of articles describing practices of this kind relating to childbirth.) These circumstances probably are strongly influenced by the facts that plantation employees have steady incomes with which to pay medical fees and have medical services available conveniently and cheaply.

The diet of plantation Filipinos leans heavily toward native Philippine dishes. Probably no Filipino of the community is unacquainted with the common American foods served in restaurants, but the general practice is to "eat Filipino." Some women state that they prefer Filipino food because it is easier to prepare. Young adults may have cosmopolitan diets which include Chinese, Hawaiian, Japanese, and European-derived foods, but the Philippine foods of their parents predominate.

Although most families have owned electric ranges with ovens for the last decade or so, foods are chiefly fried, simmered, or boiled in traditional Philippine style. Young women learn American cooking in school, and they may also learn from cookbooks and at University of Hawaii Extension Division classes conducted monthly in the community. Steamed rice remains the chief item of diet. Other representative dishes are stews of vegetables and meat, most frequently pork.

Many vegetable ingredients of Philippine dishes that may not ordinarily or easily be purchased are grown by individual householders. Varieties of beans and peas seldom used by other peoples of Hawaii are raised. The tendrils, leaves, and blossoms of other plants are combined with tomato, green peppers, garlic, ginger, chili pepper, and other familiar spices. Blossoms of squash, pumpkin, *katuday* (sesbania tree), and *malungay* (horseradish tree) are added to soups and vegetable dishes. Sweet potato leaves, as well as the tuber itself, are commonly cooked and eaten. Unripe papayas and mangoes may be added to soups and stews. Bitter melon (balsam pear) is cultivated and may sometimes be gathered from volunteer growths in old pineapple fields. In former times, before effective chemical weed killers came into use, Filipinos working in the pineapple fields are said to have deliberately planted or scattered seeds of bitter melon and tomatoes from their lunches. After Filipino workmen had supposedly removed the weeds from a pineapple field, it was sometimes necessary to send crews of

Japanese workmen to cut down bitter melon and tomato vines, which the Filipino workmen would not destroy. Fields of old pineapple plants near the end of their usefulness were often densely overgrown with bitter melon vines and tomato plants producing fruit the size of cherries.

Fish, usually fried, and often fried before incorporation in stewlike dishes, is eaten frequently. Heads of fish are stewed and the eyes are considered a delicacy by some persons. *Bagoong,* small fish of various species which have been salted and preserved in jars in fairly moist form, is especially liked by Ilocanos as a condiment or minor ingredient used to flavor many dishes.

Meat, which for most persons was not everyday fare during their years in the Philippines, has high social prestige. For wedding feasts or other elaborate banquets, pork, beef, and chicken may each be prepared in several different ways. Beef is sometimes used raw in dishes which include vinegar and spices. Blood is the principal ingredient of some dishes, to which vinegar, spices, and vegetables are added.

Filipino dishes are seldom relished by members of other ethnic groups in the community, a circumstance of which Filipinos are well aware. A wedding feast, to which non-Filipinos may be invited, usually excludes blood dishes. Other Philippine foods which strike non-Filipinos as being barbaric and loathsome, such as the nearly hatched embryos of chickens, are seldom eaten in Maunaloa. The custom of eating dogs, which had once almost vanished but was revived in 1946 when new Ilocanos came from the Philippines, seems doomed to extinction in the near future.

Philippine cuisine, except that served at banquets, is a mystery about which non-Filipinos have little curiosity. Its social prestige is very low. Few non-Filipinos in the community would prepare such a dish, delicious-sounding if it appeared on the menu of a fine restaurant, as chicken broth containing cubes of green papaya (a fruit "properly" eaten only when ripe). It is interesting to note also that Philippine cuisine seems to have little status anywhere in the world outside its home ground. One finds no restaurants featuring Philippine food for tourists or the general public even in the city of Honolulu.

Comparative social status is a matter to which Filipino sensibilities are keenly attuned. Pleasure, another important aspect of life, may be linked with it in various ways. Filipinos spend much of their money on diversions and on conspicuous consumption to enhance or maintain their social status. Prestige derived or maintained in this way appears to be much more important to married men and their families than to single men. Modern conveniences for the home tend to be viewed as social necessities by husbands and wives. Single men, many of whom might better afford these luxuries than men with families, may and usually do exist without cars or television and, with no feeling of social inferiority, use two-burner kerosene stoves. (It is reported, however, that a few single men have electric ranges which they keep immaculately clean for the admiration of themselves and others, but do their cooking on the kerosene stoves.) The ownership of a large number of fighting cocks is a pleasurable hobby and at the same time confers social prestige, especially if one's birds win many bouts.

Some men, principally the unmarried, take great pride in their wardrobe, and spend much of their income on dress clothes. In extreme cases the room of a single man may resemble a miniature warehouse, containing a closet full of clothing and rows of additional garments suspended by hangers from the ceiling of the bedroom so that movement is restricted to a narrow passage between door and bed. Perhaps partly because occasions to dress in fine clothes are not frequent, a man may change clothing several times during an evening of dancing if he can conveniently reach his room. Cosmetics displayed in pretty bottles— cologne, perfume, hair pomade, and lotions—are prized by some men.

To maintain her status a married woman must have a television set, an electric stove, a washing machine, a telephone, "good" furniture, and a family automobile. If she is fairly young, she should have attractive clothing, and her daughters should be well dressed. It is also desirable that her husband have a better-than-laborer job.

"Generosity" in the form of lavish spending for the presumable benefit of others is another source of prestige for both men and women. The satisfactions of wild extravagance do not necessarily end with the moment, but may continue to cast a warm glow in retrospect. One old Filipino loves to recall the moment of glory in his youth when he reserved all the dances of a Honolulu taxi-dancer for one evening by paying her the sum of $200. To label this merely fruitless extravagance is to ignore the lasting rewards it has brought. The sum has been repaid over and over again in the pleasure of endless recountings of the tale to friends and acquaintances.

An important way of spending money which emphasizes social strivings rather than direct pleasure or comfort is for feasts and ceremonies associated with the crises of life. The bigger the party, the greater the glory. Economic conditions much improved over prewar times are reflected in these affairs. Baptismal parties have become banquets to which hundreds of people may be invited. Some families have taken over the Hawaiian custom of holding a feast ("baby *luau*") when a child reaches its first birthday. The Hawaiian *kalua* pig, a whole pig roasted in the earth by means of hot stones, and other Hawaiian foods are commonly served at such banquets.

According to established custom, Filipino weddings are grand affairs. To reflect proper credit on all the persons involved, the modern Maunaloa ceremony entails great expenditure. The bride and groom are attended by a large party, including several bridesmaids and ushers. Members of the bridal party ordinarily wear conventional American wedding attire. The bride usually wears a white bridal gown of American style. A very few girls have the good fortune to be married in formal Filipino costume. These handsome gowns, with their ballooned, diaphanous sleeves, are highly coveted but much more expensive than American wedding dresses. A banquet in the Filipino clubhouse customarily follows the ceremony. When feasting has ended, the bride and groom lead the dancing to a hired orchestra, usually one of the two amateur Filipino bands of the community. The Philippine custom of throwing coins to the bride and groom as they initiate the dancing is still sometimes observed.

According to custom, the groom provides the bride's dress, earrings (a traditional and important part of the costume) and additional accessories, and bears all the other nuptial expenses. The increasing costs of a wedding are now often shared by the two families, who may have to spend their entire savings. But the social pressures to make it a grand affair are very strong.

Funerals also have recently become occasions for vast and conspicuous expenditure. The death of a plantation employee formerly meant a simple ceremony and interment in the community cemetery at the edge of the pineapple fields in a simple pine box made, free of charge, by plantation carpenters. The principal expense to Filipino families was a few dollars for food for the mourners. Coffins and embalmment by a professional undertaker have now been added, and funeral feasts have become more elaborate. Expenses for a "proper" funeral run as high as a thousand dollars. Few can afford such expenditures, but, as with wedding festivities, social pressures to follow the newly established customs are very forceful.

As we have seen, the cultural backgrounds and other circumstances of the Filipinos of Maunaloa vary greatly. It is not easy to generalize about them, but certain attitudes are displayed by most persons in the group. Filipino conceptions of the good life are much closer to those of Hawaiians and Cosmopolitans than to those of Japanese and Haoles.

The world of Maunaloa Filipinos is not a grim place where man should toil unremittingly. The Protestant ethic is not the native Filipino mode of thought; no great virtue attaches to the man of unflagging industry and thrift. Pleasure is one of the greatest rewards of life, but its quest is not a matter of self-conscious pursuit or desperate striving. Pleasure comes naturally and easily, in warm human relations, in games and other diversions, and in the comforts which money can buy. Prestige gained from money is important, but the pursuit of money is not an end in itself. It is a means whereby one gains what is necessary and some of what is desirable in life.

These—it must be added—are attitudes which are being displaced by American counterparts. They are much less evident among the Hawaii-born than among their parents. A close correlation seems to exist between success as a plantation employee and the degree of retention or loss of these Philippine values. The Filipinos who hold the best plantation jobs (and, consequently, the highest prestige) are the men who in these and all other ways are the most Americanized.

V | *The Japanese*

Although they are far outnumbered by Filipinos, employees of Japanese descent nevertheless form the backbone of the plantation. Twenty-two of the fifty hold salaried positions, of which all except a few clerical posts held by young women carry considerable authority. The several male Japanese heads of households who are not in plantation employ also hold positions—as postmaster, store proprietor, and schoolteacher —regarded as substantial. Superior to the Filipinos in formal education and, on the average, farther removed in time from the ancestral native culture, most of the Japanese are well adjusted to American ways of life. To refer to them as Japanese is, in fact, unwarranted; nearly all are American citizens and conduct themselves as such.

The Japanese do not form a truly united group. Many factors serve to hold them apart, as these factors prevent other peoples of the community from becoming tightly knit units. One gets the impression that the Japanese consider a united front as somehow unpatriotic, unethical, and undesirable, and feel that they have no reason to unite for mutual advantage or to meet any common threat. Despite the antagonism in the United States during World War II toward persons of Japanese ancestry, no discernible local opposition to them, as Japanese, exists today as a threat to bring unity through defense.

Residents of Japanese ancestry are well aware that they hold responsible, well-paid positions, that much of the burden of community affairs rests upon their backs, and that they are well regarded in the community and the whole of Hawaii. They know also that their racial background imposes some limitation on their social and occupational attainments. But they seem to accept these circumstances with good grace, or even happily as improvements over conditions of the past.

An in-group feeling unquestionably exists—Japanese in plantation communities seldom marry anyone but Japanese—but many distinctions are made among themselves. Intra-Japanese groupings depend upon occupational rank, and, in lesser degree, kinship (many families are related genetically or through ties of marriage), shared interests, and personal likes and dislikes. Differences in culture between the aged Japanese nationals and the younger Americans of Japanese ancestry hold the young and the old apart, but among kinfolk the relationships are close and warm. Ethnocentric attitudes of the inherent inferiority of Japanese from Okinawa also serve in waning degree to preserve social distances.

The 134 Japanese of the community comprise thirty-one married couples of which both husband and wife are Japanese, two Japanese wives of non-Japanese men, two each of aged widows and widowers, a half-dozen young single men, and sixty children.

Like the Filipinos, the Japanese of the community are difficult to characterize in a collective sense because of many cultural differences associated with education, plantation position, and place of birth. Certain generalizations may, however, be made for both issei and nisei adults. Some of these statements undoubtedly apply or will apply also to the children of Japanese descent, nearly all of whom are sansei (the second generation of American-born).

Economically the Japanese are well favored. All except a handful of aged Japanese nationals hold semiskilled, skilled, and administrative or supervisory positions. Ordinarily they miss work only when serious illness or some major crisis makes absence necessary. Even the few men and women who work as field laborers earn good wages by unfailing appearance when work is offered. Most of the Japanese have savings accounts in banks, and are very economical in household management.

Thrift does not mean that Maunaloa Japanese do without. Almost every family owns an automobile, a television set, and modern electrical appliances. Unlike Haoles, who have good incomes but whether thrifty or not have many obligatory expenses, the Japanese are both thrifty and able to practice economy. Their diet is a mixture of American, Japanese, and "Hawaiian" foods, with emphasis on inexpensive rice and less emphasis on expensive meats. Little is spent on alcoholic beverages, and expenses for entertainment and many other things are much lower than those of Haoles.

Only the younger and more recently employed supervisory employees of Japanese ancestry have attended college, but probably all Japanese parents desire a college education for their children. Before World War II, higher education was beyond reach because of the low wages prevailing. College training became an attainable goal at the end of the war, and since that time about half of the eligible nisei of both sexes have attended or are attending college.

Orderliness and social conformity are outstanding characteristics of the Japanese. In standards of morality and ethics they have the highest rating. Sexual immorality is rare, and crime among them is virtually nonexistent. Their homes, regardless of income, are neat and clean.

THE ISSEI

The eleven men and five women of the community who were born in Japan are the remnants of a group which was formerly much larger. Nearly all are aged or of advanced middle age. Culturally identifiable with the issei—and so regarded by younger Japanese and all other residents of the community—are several middle-aged or elderly Hawaii-born women of Japanese descent who are wives of issei. Raised in traditional Japanese style, they are hardly distinguishable in speech and attitude from their Japan-born mates.

The issei are not socially united, and, except for having provided sons and daughters who have remained at Maunaloa, are of little importance in community affairs. Speaking English imperfectly or not at all, they are still rather strongly oriented toward Japanese ways of life. Most of these men and women were born and spent their childhood in prefectures of southern Honshu and Kyushu, but others come from northeastern Japan and from Okinawa, regions distant in location, and diverse in speech and customs. This diversity in their backgrounds tends to make them alien to each other in the Maunaloa community.

The greatest social distinction which these men and women draw among themselves refers to those of Okinawan birth, who are regarded as inferior by other Japanese and are socially excluded. These circumstances apply also in Japan in places where Okinawans, who are relatively few in number and geographically far removed from the large cities of Japan proper, have come into contact with "real" Japanese. Discrimination is much more prevalent in Hawaii, however, as a relatively large proportion of laborers imported from Japan came from Okinawa. Among the issei of Hawaii, social exclusion of Okinawans has usually been firm, and marriage of their children to the offspring of Okinawan parents is bitterly opposed. Many marriages of this sort have, however, taken place within the past two decades in Hawaii and some within the community of Maunaloa.

To determine the strength of anti-Okinawan feeling today is a difficult task. "Real" Japanese will often discuss the subject freely. The aged express strong prejudice; the young say they feel little or none. But even among the young who deny prejudice, telltale evidence of its existence crops up in expressions such as "those people." Okinawans and the descendants of Okinawans are reluctant to discuss the matter, or else they deny that they have ever suffered active discrimination.

We may say with certainty, however, that anti-Okinawan prejudice still exists but is decreasing. Although the issei have bent little, the young tend to minimize the social gap and, in the words of one nisei, "go more by the individual." In former times many difficulties in personal relations were the lot of plantation Okinawans or their children who rose to positions of authority over Japanese from the islands of Japan proper. Today an educated young man of Okinawan parentage is accepted on terms of apparent social equality by many of the younger Japanese in positions of authority, and this acceptance serves as a model for Japanese who otherwise might adhere to the old ways.

Like their countrymen in Japan, most issei are both Buddhists and Shintoists, but they have abandoned many of the supernaturalistic beliefs ("folk" Shinto) of the rural areas of Japan from which they came. Some still maintain votary shelves (*kamidana*) in their homes for Shinto deities, to whom they make daily offerings of foodstuffs. They may also observe the most important of the events of the Shinto ceremonial calendar. But these beliefs and practices are difficult to maintain in an atmosphere dominated by people of other culture and by offspring who know little or nothing of the significance of the supernatural beings and the ritual acts involved.

According to beliefs prevailing in Japan from ancient times, dangerous pollution was incurred by contact with blood in any form and with death. In extreme form the taboos required the isolation of women during menses and prohibition against their making prayers or offerings to the *kamisama* (Shinto deities) during these times.

Restrictions placed upon women at childbirth were still greater. They were isolated for a period of thirty-three days after parturition. A woman under the taboos following childbirth might not step into the sun with uncovered head for fear of offending the Sun Goddess, and she must, for the same reason, hang the newly washed clothing of herself and her infant to dry in the shade rather than in direct sunlight. Gradually she resumed her former social relations with others and with the *kamisama* as pollution diminished with time. Rites of purification involving the use of salt and water and the kindling of ceremonial fires were also required.

Death was the most serious source of pollution, which extended to close relatives of the deceased. The taboos applying to death pollution were the strictest of all.

The themes of pollution and purification remain today as the core of Shintoism. The custom of isolating the polluted to prevent contamination of others is still followed in modified form in much of rural Japan. Shinto beliefs and practices were brought over from Japan to Hawaii in diverse form according to the local versions of the regions from which the migrants came. They have been maintained in Hawaii in varying and much-diminished degree—menstrual taboos seem to have been the first to disappear—but have seldom been communicated to Hawaii-born offspring.

As in Japan, Buddhism is important as the religion of death. Buddhist memorial tablets (*ihai*) bearing the posthumous names of the deceased are customarily kept in the homes, and the Buddhist ceremonials surrounding death are observed, less strictly perhaps than in Japan. Issei faithfully contribute money toward the maintenance of the Buddhist temple on the island, where they may attend traditional ceremonies. Buddhist ceremonial procedures are carried out in the home also. But confusion may exist in regard to ritual. Many Buddhist sects exist in Japan, and they differ in beliefs and practices. The issei of the community belonged to a number of different sects at the time of their arrival in Hawaii, but Buddhism is officially represented on Molokai by one priest and one sect, the Sōdō subsect of Zen. For lack of opportunity to continue the faiths in which they were reared, issei have become affiliated with this alien sect.

Supernaturalistic beliefs which fall outside the ordinary realms of Buddhism and sect or shrine Shinto exist, but they have little influence on community life, since the number who hold them is small. Ghosts and monsters of various kinds fall into the realm of half-belief, as do old ideas of bewitchment and possession by spirits. More important, however, are the magical practices associated with childbirth and death, and observances to avoid calamity during certain critical years.

Old Japanese customs of exuvial magic at childbirth concerned with the placenta and umbilical cord were transplanted to Hawaii and, as already noted, had a long life in the community of Maunaloa. According to rural customs in Japan, the placenta was buried in the earth floor of the dwelling after the birth of a male infant, especially a first-born male, to insure that he remain at home (and continue the family line) after reaching adulthood. For a girl, burial of the placenta outside the entrance of the house insured that she follow the proper procedure of marrying out of the family upon reaching maturity. These practices were difficult to follow in Hawaii, but placentas were commonly buried somewhere. As in Japan, the umbilical cord was kept for possible future use as medicine or with the idea of burial with the person concerned upon his death. In Hawaii as well as in modern Japan, the cords may be wrapped and put away, but usually the location of the tiny pieces of dried organic matter is eventually forgotten.

Ancient Japanese customs surround the *yakudoshi,* certain years of life which are believed to be inherently critical, years in which calamity is likely to befall or fortunes to change sharply. The critical years are variously interpreted. In most of Japan they are the forty-second for males and the thirty-third for females. Similar beliefs in Okinawa refer to quite different years and entail different ceremonials. Most persons believe that *yakudoshi* must be reckoned in traditional Japanese fashion, whereby an individual is one year old at birth and becomes a year older at the beginning of each calendrical new year. To avoid calamity during the *yakudoshi,* offerings to deities requesting their intercession may be made by the persons concerned and by relatives. Sometimes parties are held to which friends and relatives are invited. Above all, the person in *yakudoshi* must avoid any major decision that might seriously affect his future life, and must not undertake long and potentially dangerous trips.

The beliefs and practices of *yakudoshi* have been remarkably viable in modern Japan, and are common today among even sophisticated urban Japanese. They exist also in Hawaii, but in far more haphazard fashion. Both believers and disbelievers are found among the issei of Maunaloa. In this as in other aspects of life, however, the issei residents of Honolulu probably lean more to the traditional Japanese customs than do the Japan-born residents of plantation communities.

Another realm of supernaturalism important in Japan during the youth of the issei and still flourishing in rural Japan today has dwindled to the point of near-disappearance at Maunaloa. Excluding prayer, magico-religious techniques of treating disease are almost entirely absent.

Religion, language, and diet are the areas of life in which the issei have retained Japanese customs to the greatest degree, but in none of these matters are they wholly Japanese. Two couples who returned to Japan for a visit in 1956 after many years in Hawaii reported bewilderment at customs and great linguistic difficulty in communicating with their relatives and other former countrymen. So many Hawaiian and especially English words had unconsciously become included in their presumably Japanese speech, they stated, that they were seldom fully understood, and they, in turn, had forgotten so many Japanese words that they often failed to understand the speech of their hosts.

The diet of these "elderly" Japanese is mixed. Japanese foods are the most important, but American foods are included also. The major American additions are meat and chicken, which are seldom a part of the rural Japanese diet because of their high cost and probably also because of the lingering effect of old Buddhist prohibitions against eating the flesh of animals. The alcoholic beverages chiefly used are whisky and beer. Sake, the rice "wine" of Japan, has become uncommon in the community since the beginning of World War II, which inhibited many traditional Japanese customs.

Clothing worn in public is invariably Western, with the occasional exception, chiefly among women, of Japanese *zori*, or sandals. *Zori* are the most common footgear in one's own yard and for brief trips or informal calls. *Geta*, high wooden clogs, are sometimes worn about the yard in rainy weather. As is true of virtually all except Haole homes, no footgear except stockings is worn inside the dwelling. Within their homes, issei men still sometimes wear *yukata*, cotton garments of the "kimono" type, after they have returned from work and bathed.

A hot bath rather than a shower remains for the issei one of the comforts of life which they should not be denied. In times gone by, before toilet and bath facilities were installed in each plantation dwelling, separate bathhouses of Japanese style for men and for women were

maintained for residents of the "camps." They could then soak pleas-
urably in the hot water of the fairly large tubs. If many people used the
same water, it was a matter of little concern to those accustomed to this
practice in Japan. Much grumbling is said to have emanated from the
issei, people little given to complaining to the management, when the
communal tubs were replaced by home showers. The installation of
bathtubs in the homes resolved the issue.

The giving of gifts, a Japanese custom surrounded by well-defined
rules of etiquette and reciprocity, remains a custom for some issei despite strong local opposition from nisei and from plantation officials.
Following Japanese custom, gifts are given at New Year's, when making social calls, when someone is ill, and on numerous other occasions.
The recipient is under strong moral obligation to reciprocate. In Hawaii, it became the custom to give one's boss a present at Christmas,
even though he might not be Japanese and thus would not reciprocate.
These gifts to supervisors were viewed as moral obligations and as
pledges of good will, although reciprocity from the superior consisted
only of the tacit assurance of his continued favor and good will. Gifts
to supervisory employees have long been prohibited by company policy,
but a few of the issei still attempt secretly to make them, and follow
the custom among themselves. Under the compulsion of this ancient
Japanese custom, one old employee annually unburdens himself of his
moral debt to the plantation manager, who refuses to accept gifts, by
the successful stratagem of presenting the manager's wife with a bottle
of whisky at Christmas. In amusement and understanding, the gift is
accepted.

Culturally neither wholly Japanese nor American, the issei of the
community have made workable compromises in adjusting to the ways
of Hawaii. No characteristic patterns of entertainment exist, and no
conspicuous longing for things Japanese is evident. Social activities of
a Japanese nature include occasional Japanese movies in Kaunakakai
(once regularly scheduled at the theater at Maunaloa but abandoned
because of waning attendance as the issei dwindled in numbers) and
some participation in Buddhist ceremonials. Bon dancing, a presumably
religious ceremonial which might better be described as entertainment,
attracts issei to Kaunakakai as participants or observers. More folk
dance than serious ritual, dancing at Bon (the annual midsummer
Buddhist festival honoring the dead) was revived after the war and is

popular principally among issei and small children of Japanese ancestry. Fishing, picnics at the beach, attendance at school affairs in which their grandchildren are participants, watching television, and other customary "American" forms of recreation are also enjoyed.

The life and thoughts of the issei revolve about their children, most of whom are mature and themselves parents, and their grandchildren. Few wish to follow Japanese tradition and live with their children upon retirement, but familial relations are close and warm. Although vanishing, the issei leave behind them an enormous progeny and also leave among these descendants a foreign cultural inheritance whose depth is difficult to measure.

THE NISEI

If the term "nisei" is interpreted strictly to mean the American-born sons and daughters of Japanese men and women born in Japan, the age range of Maunaloa nisei is great. A few Hawaii-born women well past fifty years of age, who are culturally issei, would be included, as would a few children. The term "nisei" will be used here to describe a rather clearly distinguishable group of Hawaii-born adults of Japanese ancestry, one or both of whose parents were born in Japan. Within this group no readily observable differences exist between persons whose parents were both issei and the smaller number of persons who are the offspring of issei-nisei unions.

The term "nisei" implies much more than a kind of biogeographical classification. The forty-odd adults placed under this heading are culturally distinct in many important ways from their elders of Japanese descent. Their pasts, their futures, and the futures of their children lie in America, and their modes of life are strongly, sometimes consciously, oriented to follow American patterns. These men and women are vital to both plantation and community. Nisei assume most of the responsibility for community affairs. They are importantly represented in the community council, the federal credit union, the university extension club, the parent-teacher association, the Boy Scouts, Girl Scouts, athletic clubs, and local branches of political parties and other organizations whose membership extends beyond the confines of the community.

Maunaloa nisei are prominent also in communal affairs of the island, such as the community chest, directorship of the community hospital, and the island chamber of commerce. In only one organization, the local branch of the labor union, do nisei seem reluctant to assume positions of responsibility, apparently because of a feeling that the union is not wholly desirable and that appointment to union officership somehow puts the individual in an unfavorable position with relation to "the company." Some nisei express the view that union officership is a thankless task, involving only work and responsibility of an administrative sort without real participation or influence in decisions. No nisei of the community belongs to any organization whose membership is confined to persons of Japanese descent.

It is not surprising that nisei should play such an important part in community affairs. They comprise the largest group of active, ablebodied men and women who possess the qualifications necessary for leadership. Better-educated than any other sizable group except the Haoles, they have generally had at least a high-school education, and are thus equipped to meet the demands of literacy and of social presence which officialdom requires. This longer period of formal education and concomitantly longer exposure to the American middle-class standards projected by schoolteachers has been important in instilling the ideas that responsibility in communal relations is appropriate, desirable, and morally obligatory. Some nisei explain that they are "communityminded," whereas Filipinos are not. Participation in communal affairs is, to be sure, strongly developed in rural Japan (a circumstance of which the Maunaloa nisei are probably unaware). It appears unlikely, however, that this attitude or proclivity has been passed on from issei parents, who on the plantations of Hawaii have not been active in community matters. A few nisei say that participation in community affairs might help a man in his work, but others strongly disagree.

Although American attitudes and customs are dominant among the nisei, it could hardly be expected that the years of exposure in childhood to the Japanese culture of parents and elders would have no effect. Maunaloa nisei, in fact, represent a composite of the two cultures, and their lives also reflect local influences stemming from the nature of plantation community life. An accurate appraisal of the ratio of Japanese and American components in the culture of these nisei is far beyond the aims of this study. Many attitudes and values are unspoken and elusive, difficult to determine without refined techniques of observation.

What is Japanese about the nisei in all except covert attitudes or values is fairly simple to see or learn. Clothing is almost entirely American except for sandals (*zori*) worn on informal occasions. As a matter of fact, *zori* ceased long ago to be distinctively Japanese, and are common among Hawaiian residents of any racial or cultural background. Wooden clogs are occasionally worn to water plants or to do laundry on the back porch or in the yard. Nisei women are generally fastidious about their appearance and are careful to be well groomed in public under even the most informal circumstances.

Diet is extremely varied, including Chinese-derived dishes (popular among many residents of Hawaii), Japanese, and, especially, American foods. For most households, rice is indispensable. As many nisei express it, a meal without rice somehow leaves them feeling "as if something had been left out." Other Japanese foods include *udon* (noodles), *tempura* (fish, shellfish, or vegetables dipped in a light batter and deep-fried), *daikon* (pickled radish), *heka* (the usual name in Hawaii for what is customarily called *sukiyaki* in Japan—a food which rural people of Japan can rarely afford), *sashimi* (raw fish of certain species), *mochi* (sticky cakes of glutenous rice which may contain a filling of sweetened paste made from beans), and *sushi* (cold cooked rice in which pieces of vegetables or other foods may be mixed, the whole enclosed in a cover of fried bean curd). Fish, prepared in either Japanese or Western style, is popular, but the supply of fish, as elsewhere in Hawaii, is poor and the price is high.

Lest the foregoing inventory create the impression of a strong leaning toward Japanese foods, it should be added that common Western foods are dominant in the diet. Nisei housewives are sometimes avid collectors of recipes for new dishes. Alcoholic beverages consumed are whisky and beer, generally in moderate quantities. Nisei women rarely drink anything alcoholic.

Amusements of the nisei bear no apparent relation to Japanese pursuits, with the possible exception of baseball, long extremely popular among males in Japan. There is also little social dancing: in Japanese tradition, physical contact with others in public is avoided. Few nisei of the community have learned ballroom dancing—but few opportunities to learn this accomplishment were available during their youth. Some young women and girls take lessons in the hula, and nisei women may occasionally participate in Bon dancing. Mah-jong is a favorite diversion among men in the highest-ranking occupations. Mah-jong groups include non-Japanese of equal occupational rank. Diversions are otherwise the familiar American and modern Hawaiian ones of bridge, movies, television, gardening, picnics, fishing, familiar sports, and school activities.

The men's golf club, open to all persons of the community who wish to join, is composed principally of nisei supervisors, whose wives are prominent in the much smaller women's golf club. Nisei members of the golf club are predominantly those who hold superior positions on the plantation, and club membership is regarded as an insignia of social elevation. Bridge is, in similar fashion, important to women as a mark of social status.

Maunaloa nisei are rarely proficient in the Japanese language. All learned to speak it with varying degrees of skill in childhood, but most today are unable to converse in pure Japanese. When it is necessary to speak with issei, many resort to a combination of Japanese, English, and Hawaiian words which are placed in a Japanese linguistic frame-work. All of them were taught how to write in Japanese. They received this training for several years in Japanese language schools which were conducted every afternoon after the sessions of the public schools of Hawaii had ended. Teaching of this kind was prohibited at the begin-ning of World War II, but the present adult nisei of the community are old enough to have received several years of instruction. Some persons who had studied Japanese for many years attained a fairly high degree of proficiency in reading and writing, and were able to read newspapers, magazines, and books in Japanese, accomplishments which require years of study even in Japan. During World War II this was strongly disapproved as being unpatriotic, and, moreover, the supply of new literature was cut off.

The several thousand Chinese-derived ideographs used in writing Japanese are quickly forgotten unless the memory is refreshed by re-peated exposure to them. Today few if any nisei are capable of reading Japanese books without halting and referring frequently to dictionaries. Most nisei remember part of the two phonetic scripts of Japanese (phonetically identical and comparable with cursive writing and print-ing of the English alphabet), which are ordinarily used in combination with the Chinese ideographs for verbal inflections and to represent ele-ments of the Japanese language which cannot be expressed in the nonphonetic Chinese ideographs. Generally, however, competence in spoken Japanese is not great and competence in writing is near the zero mark.

But nisei of the community consider at least some acquaintance with the Japanese language to be desirable. The teaching of Japanese was resumed in 1955, with the Buddhist priest serving as teacher. Nearly all nisei have enrolled their children for this training, although some of the children, with the approval of their parents, have ceased to attend classes for lack of interest. Classes are conducted once a week for an hour. Even twenty years of faithful attendance, however, would never result in proficiency in written Japanese unless the student did much independent work. It seems reasonable to state that the sansei, the present generation of children, will include no individuals who as adults have genuine mastery of spoken and written Japanese.

The Japanese language has given way also in practices of naming children; the trend has long been toward the selection of European names. Nisei customarily have two given names, one Japanese and the other European, but usually they are known and addressed by their European name. Sometimes issei parents use the Japanese name but other persons use the European. Children of nisei may be named in the same fashion, but the tendency is increasingly toward two European names. Names selected are quite conventional—and thus form a sharp contrast with the fanciful and elegant given names of many Filipino and Cosmopolitan children.

Most nisei are nominal Buddhists, who, like their elders, contribute toward the support of the Buddhist priest and temple at Kaunakakai. Such donations appear to be viewed in the same light as taxes and contributions to the community chest and other charities, obligations which should be faithfully met. Few nisei know more than the merest fragments of Buddhist dogma and their participation in Buddhist ceremonial is extremely slight. Many nisei who identify themselves as Buddhists do not know the name of the sect to which they officially belong—it is to them merely "Buddhist"—and, although children might be taken to the outdoor Bon dances, traditional ceremonies at the temple are seldom attended. New Year's, a period of great ceremonial activity in Japan, means to most Maunaloa nisei only that rice cakes and perhaps other traditional foods should be served.

The rites of Buddhism are important, in form at least, in connection with death. Funerals are conducted by the Buddhist priest, and some of the many prescribed memorial ceremonies are customarily observed. The full roster of commemorative services on the anniversary of death is probably observed by no one. The children of nisei are exposed even less than their parents to Buddhist ideology and ritual, and it appears likely that, whether or not they regard themselves as Buddhists upon reaching maturity, they will have little knowledge of the religion.

Shinto is even less well known to the nisei, who tend to look down upon these beliefs of their parents in a tolerant fashion. Nisei know or remember that their parents had votary shelves for the *kamisama* which contained ritual objects, including dishes for offerings and sometimes figurines representing the deities, and that certain rituals were observed before the shelves. The identity of the deities, however, is often unknown. (Many thousands of deities exist in the loosely formed pantheon of Shinto.) Some nisei recall references to a god of the stove, to the Sun-Goddess Amaterasu-o-mikami, to the Fox-God Inarisama, and to various other well-known figures of Shinto. The term "Shinto," however, conveys virtually no meaning to them. Middle-aged nisei women often have a fleeting acquaintance with traditional Japanese beliefs concerning pollution at childbirth. Some can recall that their mothers advised them, on the birth of their first child, that they should avoid certain foods and should "rest" for thirty-three days. A very few persons among the nisei are acquainted with purificatory rites, and might still follow such practices as sprinkling salt. To many others these practices are unknown, and would doubtless be viewed as old-fashioned curiosities.

Many nisei recall hearing, in childhood, tales of ghosts and monsters, and of good and bad luck, which they refer to as "superstitions." Some are familiar with the beliefs of *yakudoshi* and state that, whereas to their knowledge no nisei of the community holds them, they are current among nisei in Honolulu. Some younger nisei know nothing about such beliefs. As with other matters of native Japanese culture, familiarity is strongly correlated with age. Older nisei, who were generally raised in a home atmosphere closer to that of Japan, are better acquainted with Japanese culture and retain it more strongly than do their juniors.

A number of nisei are members of Protestant churches, which they joined as adults. A few declare themselves to be agnostics. Whether Buddhist or Christian, most persons have recourse to religion only on special occasions, principally funerals.

Certain other Japanese customs appear to retain a half-life because the parents of the nisei observe them. Infants, just after birth, may receive gifts of Japanese clothing from their grandparents, but almost never on other occasions. These gifts might be donned once, to please their donors. Girls may receive Japanese dolls from their grandparents on Girls' Day. The inflated paper carp, a traditional feature of Boys' Day in Japan, has not been seen in Maunaloa since the beginning of World War II.

The Japanese elements that remain in nisei weddings are partly attributable to the presence of Japan-born parents. No nisei wedding of Japanese style has been held in the community since the beginning of World War II, and at that time American ceremonies had already begun to replace the Japanese. A wedding feast and party today, however, still include Japanese foods and the singing of Japanese songs by aged males, in a traditionally intoxicated state from drinking untraditional whisky. Issei have long favored frosted layer cakes and soft drinks, which are served along with Japanese foods at a wedding feast.

The degree of survival of Japanese attitudes and values of other kinds is much more difficult to estimate. Certainly, as among the people of Japan, the nisei tend to be punctilious in meeting obligations, and one can always expect full reciprocity for kindnesses or services extended them.

As in Japan, social distances are preserved. Place and its prerogatives are important, and one keeps his place. Behavior toward one's superiors is very respectful. The "boss" (the plantation manager) is highly respected, in his absence as well as in his presence. Personal loyalty to the manager appears most marked among the Japanese, suggesting the influence of Japanese tradition, but this attitude appears to be prevalent among all peoples of Hawaiian plantations, both sugar and pineapple, probably as a heritage from the paternalistic atmosphere of early Hawaiian plantation life.

In patterns of familial authority and unity, some of the traditional Japanese ways are clearly retained. Husbands and wives associate freely and customarily in public, but the husband is the undisputed master of the household, and the affairs of any member of the family tend to be viewed as the affairs of all.

Following the pattern of Japan, the nisei seem to feel the sanctions of ridicule more strongly than others in the community. Any criticism, whether satirical or not, is likely to be taken very seriously, and reprimand in the presence of others constitutes disgrace.

The transition from the Japanese culture of their parents to a predominantly and increasingly American way of life has for many nisei been a "natural," insensible process involving little emotional disturbance. For others, especially the innovators in acceptance of American customs, transition has meant struggle and unhappiness. During World War II, only echoes of anti-Japanese prejudice reached the Japanese of Maunaloa. Some state that they disliked to be called "Buddha-head," an opprobrious term used especially during the war for persons of Japanese ancestry, and at this time they also became acutely aware of their Japanese customs. Children also were said to have become conscious of the wartime anti-Japanese attitudes, although they were mild throughout Hawaii and least strong in settled small communities such as Maunaloa. Some are said to have told their parents that they "did not want to be Japanese."

At the time of the attack on Pearl Harbor some issei felt it necessary to voice their allegiance to America. One old woman paid me a special visit on December 8, 1941, to explain her stand: "S'pose steal-man come, I speak take. S'pose Japanee come, me I like fight." [I would not resist a robber, but I would fight invading Japanese.] Most issei and nisei were silent, but expressed their partisanship by continued peaceful coöperation and by patriotic effort. After December 7 the sale of government bonds, handled through the plantation office, jumped mightily.

Another form of patriotism, also a sensible precaution, an insurance against censure for being "Japanese," was to eschew things Japanese. Much that was Japanese—marriage customs, traditional festivals, the formalized exchange of gifts, the wearing of Japanese clothing, and the drinking of sake—disappeared after the beginning of the war. But these changes had long been under way; the war was not the exclusive agent of change, but rather a stimulus to expedite a trend already well established.

At the onset of World War II, nisei innovators in Americanism had been active in the community for several years, in spite of the opposition of their elders. The following extracts from the reminiscences of one of the extreme innovators is representative of the cultural conflicts in the lives of many nisei of the community and of Hawaii at large.

"When I went to school, on another island, I wanted to be like all the other kids. I didn't want Japanese things and I didn't want Japanese food. My father was ditch man on a sugar plantation, and we lived in a little plantation house. They didn't pay much in those days and I wasn't the only kid, so we didn't have much money. That's the wrong way to say it—we were very poor. There were a lot of us kids and my mother had to work on the plantation too. There was a *yochi-en* [day nursery for children of plantation mothers] next door, and we stayed there sometimes so my mother could work. I used to envy the other kids in school for the kind of food they ate. We had Japanese food, and my mother sent me to school with Japanese food for lunch, rice, the cheapest canned *tempura,* and *umeboshi* [pickled small plums]. I can't eat that *tempura* and *umeboshi* today. I hate them.

"My mother couldn't speak English, and she didn't have much of a chance to learn American ways. But somewhere she learned to make chocolate pudding, which I had had and liked. Then she made chocolate pudding every day, day after day after day. I can't stand chocolate pudding even now.

"I'm a Protestant and so is my wife. I remember when I was a kid, at New Year's, when the *shishi* [ceremonial lion; that is, men animating a grotesque lion-like head and a fabric body] came to our gate. You were supposed to put your head into its mouth and let it 'bite' you, and then you would have good luck. You were also supposed to give the *shishi* some money. I thought this was crazy, and I told the *shishi* to go away. My father was there. He didn't say anything. I know he didn't like it, but he didn't say anything.

"I did lots of things he didn't like, but he never stood in my way, and he was always good to me. But I think he did very wrong, very wrong to have so many kids when he couldn't send them to school or do the things he should for them. That was wrong of him. I told him so, one time, later. He should have had fewer children so they would have a better chance. And I think it was wrong to have so many and to expect to live with one of them when he and my mother got too old. That's the last thing in the world I want to do, live with any of my children when I grow old. I want them all to go to college. I only went to high school, and it's hard to be Japanese and have only a high-school education. I've told my kids from the time they were old enough to understand that they should go to college.

"But my father was good to me and never stood in my way. When I had troubles about doing things the American way, it was other Japanese who made it hard for me. But I went right on, and they never did cut me out. I was never ostracized. When I got married, I didn't have much money and my parents didn't have much. The old folks all wanted us to have a *nakōdo* [go-between], even after my wife and I decided to get married, and they wanted the *yuinō* [a bridal gift of considerable money in addition to symbolic and relatively inexpensive gifts, given by the groom's family to the bride's family], Japanese clothes, a big party, and all the rest. But I said nuts to that stuff. Those weddings, even then, cost about a thousand dollars. I finally did give in a little, and X acted as a kind of *nakōdo,* to make the old people happy. But he did just what I said.

"We had a Protestant wedding and a small party. And we used the money we saved to buy furniture. People thought it was wrong, and talked about it and me a lot, but I just went on my regular way and nobody avoided me or caused any trouble. In other ways I think the old people felt good toward me because I used to help them write letters in English and things like that.

"Another thing that made me mad was the gift-giving. It only caused people trouble and worry. Someone gave them a gift and they had to give something back when they needed the money for other things. I refused to take gifts, and I told everybody so. I told them not to give me anything because I wouldn't give anything back. The only people those gifts were helping were the store. When you were sick, people brought flowers or something, and then you had to send them something back. Usually it was a case of soda pop. Then there were gifts at Christmas or New Year's, and lots of others, too. The old people objected when I refused to return gifts, but one of the old ones sided with me toward the end, and then almost everyone stopped doing it. A few people still do it, but mostly it's only Christmas presents. The kids, when they receive graduation presents now, just send a card of thanks.

"There's not much that's Japanese at our house now. Of course, we take off our shoes before we go in the house, but that's only sensible here, where it's so dirty outside. Sometimes we have Japanese food, but I don't like it much. I had too much when I was a kid. But I do think that children should be obedient to their parents. That's a good thing about the Japanese. If children obey their parents, I think there is a closer relation between them.

"I'd say there are less Japanese things here than in Honolulu. In Honolulu some things have been revived a little in the last few years."

Foremost among the concerns of life of the nisei, as with their parents, is the welfare of their children. Attendance at school affairs by parents is excellent. Every boy belongs to the Boy Scouts, from eight years of age until well into adolescence. Participation in the Girl Scouts is less strong. As among their forebears in Japan, sansei children are treated with great indulgence during childhood, and seldom subjected to physical punishment. As in Japan, once a child has passed early childhood, the important social sanctions to ensure conformance to standards of behavior are the opinions and statements of others.

To what extent the sansei children may hold to Japanese culture when they mature is a question. In degree of conformance with standards (but not necessarily Japanese standards) and in patterns of authority in social relationships within and without the family it is likely that they will unconsciously reflect Japanese tradition. It seems likely, also, that even in these matters, which may justly be thought to represent Japanese cultural inheritance, the sansei will nevertheless fall within the range of ordinary American behavior.

VI | *Haoles and Cosmopolitans*

THE HAOLES

The nineteen Haole adults and eleven children in Maunaloa represent a fairly random sample of Americans. As is generally true of mainland-financed plantations of Hawaii, few of the adults were born in Hawaii. Places of birth and rearing of Maunaloa Haoles include all the major regions of the United States except the deep south. A few were born in Europe. As the trained occupational elite of the community, Haole men as a group have the best educations and the best (or promise of the best) positions, salaries, and dwellings. In certain other respects they and their wives are, and often feel, less fortunate.

The total island population of Haole adults and children probably does not exceed seventy-five. The male Haole sees his Haole co-workers throughout the day. The Haole woman sees at least her intimates among other Haole women frequently during the day. When the working day is over, their company is ordinarily the associates of the hours just past.

Exchanges of dinner and entertainment and informal visits among friends are fairly frequent. An active exchange of social invitations exists also between families of Haole men holding positions of prominence on the plantation and families of similar social position in other communities of the island. At least several times a year all adult Haoles of Maunaloa gather for dinner in each other's homes. Men who hold the best positions are obliged to entertain oftener than others. The social life of the occupationally well-placed may entail heavy expenditure for food and liquor. Communal dances, in which most Haoles of the island participate, are an established custom. During 1956 square dances were held monthly. Bridge is an important form of recreation for women, both within the community and outside it. Joint familial picnics at the beach are held throughout the year.

In the history of the plantation, turnover in employment among Haole supervisors has been great. Aside from personal reasons for resignation and departure, certain serious disadvantages of life in the community are cited repeatedly. Lonesomeness has been perhaps the most important of these. To Haoles newly arrived from Honolulu or from the mainland, the community and the island are small and confining, and they find discouragingly few Haoles with similar interests and backgrounds. Intimate association with most non-Haoles is tacitly discouraged in many ways, chiefly on occupational rather than racial grounds. But generally no imposition of sanctions is needed to prevent intimacy with any except the few occupationally and otherwise socially acceptable non-Haoles of the community; cultural differences alone are sufficiently great to set the Haoles apart.

From the standpoint of occupational rank, many nisei are socially acceptable, holding positions as good as or better than those of certain Haoles. However, the dissimilarities of nisei and Haoles are sufficient to discourage intimacy. The pastimes, customs, and interests of plantation Haoles follow familiar patterns of college-bred middle-class Americans, including the serving of cocktails or highballs to guests before dinner, social dancing, and conversation about current books and national and international affairs. In these matters, all trivial but somehow important, they ordinarily have no common meeting ground with non-Haoles. Although social intermingling of Haoles with other peoples has increased markedly over former times, differences in cultural background still inhibit intercourse. Compared with other groups in the community, Haoles are veritable sophisticated worldlings.

It is noteworthy that Haoles constitute the only socially united racial-cultural group in the community. From the standpoint of smooth operation of the plantation, this is desirable and is encouraged. Probably of greater importance in bringing about this unity, however, is the fact that the Haoles constitute a minority group, small and isolated socially and culturally from non-Haoles; thus its members must turn to each other for company.

Personal animosities with fellow Haoles exist, however, and have occasionally led to resignations. Slighting remarks or acts which might in a larger social orbit go unnoticed assume undue importance. A careless slip of the tongue expressing censure, or a slighting remark, travels swiftly, and almost every Haole knows at any given time who dislikes whom and why. The long-time Haole resident learns to proceed gingerly in any matter that might arouse dissension, and to maintain a neutral silence except among his most intimate friends. Small animosities are ordinarily well suppressed, and intra-Haole relationships are cordial for the most part.

Other problems faced by Haoles of the community are those common to other Haoles of Hawaii. One of the principal concerns is over the welfare and future of their children, who are surrounded by children of different race and different if not wholly strange or undesirable ways. Probably all Haole parents would agree that, theoretically at least, their children should mingle and become acquainted with other children. This conforms with the American ideal of democracy, and Haole parents may sincerely hold this ideal. Haole children ordinarily attend the local grammar school, participate in Boy Scout or Girl Scout programs, and have some friends of other racial background. (Life for the new and lone Haole boy in a class at school might, however, be difficult.)

But intimacy leads to other evils. Haole children learn Hawaiian Pidgin from their playmates and to a lesser extent from island school-teachers. Deep concern is expressed by Haole parents about this and other matters of education for their children.

Friendship with non-Haoles has still another hazard, distant but far more serious. "Probably no Haole mother in the islands has failed to think of these things." Friendship implies intimacy, which may lead to love or, even worse, marriage. Even the Haole parents most free from ethnocentrism with regard to racial distinctions agree that the welfare of their children and future grandchildren would be jeopardized by interracial marriage. One safeguard is to inculcate children with the advantages of marriage to a Haole. This may be done consciously or unconsciously. By the time they are adolescents, many children have assimilated the desired attitude through indirect learning. A second safeguard is to remove opportunities for miscegenation. In the history of the community no Haole child has passed the entire period from childhood through adolescence as a full-time resident. Parents have requested and received transfers to positions in other island communities or on the mainland, or have sent their adolescent children to school in Honolulu. Other factors beyond the fear of miscegenation are important in this connection. High-school education for boarding students is expensive; hence it is economically desirable to take employment in communities where appropriate schools are available.

The Haoles are in a curiously unfavorable economic position. Despite having by far the largest average incomes, they may be in poor financial condition. A high standard of living compared with other peoples of the community and social pressures which force them to conform with that standard keep many of the Haoles poor in spite of attempts to be thrifty. Haole women, except for the wives of the highest plantation officials, customarily do their own housework. But eggs and milk and other foods and necessities must be imported and thus are expensive. Entertainment may be costly, and the higher one's occupational rank the greater one's outlay for this purpose. The outside education of children, who as a matter of course go on to college after graduation from out-island high schools, is a heavy drain.

An additional expense, confined almost wholly to Haoles, is for periodic vacations on the mainland. These excursions are usually regarded as necessities rather than luxuries. Great effort is directed toward accumulating the funds required for such a trip, and once it is over, planning and saving begin again.

For most Haoles, life in Maunaloa is viewed as transitory, an interlude of a few years before they obtain a better job in some other community or return to the mainland. No one, of course, plans to live in Maunaloa after retirement (a physical impossibility unless increased mechanization or outright sale of corporation dwellings made housing available), and probably few would favor the idea of retiring anywhere on the island. For non-Haoles, however, continued residence in Hawaii if not in the plantation community is the normal expectation.

Although many of the circumstances described above discourage participation in community affairs by Haoles, they play a large role, chiefly as patrons, advisers, and innovators. For some, participation is viewed as an obligation which must be efficiently and faithfully discharged. For others, especially those who expect to remain for many years, interest in community and island affairs may be keen and wholehearted.

The foregoing paragraphs have referred principally to Haoles employed in supervisory and administrative capacities by the pineapple corporation. A few "outside" Haoles are also a normal part of the community. Because their employment is not with the plantation and their residence is brief, plantation Haoles tend to view them as being peripheral to the main stream of social life. Whether or not the outsiders actively participate in Haole social affairs depends primarily upon their own personalities and interests.

Outsiders have ordinarily been limited to a few female schoolteachers from the mainland, and an occasional Haole principal and his family. From long experience, plantation Haoles have come to expect a rapid turnover among these teachers. A pleasant girl who cheerfully accepts plantation life is accepted eagerly as a welcome addition to the Haole social circle, but plantation Haoles are under no compulsion to socialize with outsiders who are uncongenial or disinterested.

To the occasional mainland schoolteacher who is imbued with ideas of democracy and equality, and who has had no previous knowledge of Hawaiian social distinctions (and probably little acquaintance with counterparts on the mainland), the occupational and ethnic divisions in the community may seem disturbingly and shamefully wrong: "When I arrived at the airport, one of the first things the person who met me said was, 'Do you play bridge?' I said I didn't much like it, and this person said, 'Well, if you want to get in with the right crowd here you'll play bridge.' The things I've seen here since then [social distinctions] sometimes make me ashamed to be a Haole."

COSMOPOLITANS AND COSMOPOLITAN UNIONS

The term "Cosmopolitan," as used here, refers to persons of mixed national and cultural backgrounds according to the classification of nations and cultures conventionally recognized in Hawaii. It implies no necessary racial mixture. Among the peoples of the plantation community only one, the Hawaiian, is given the status of a distinct race in any scientific classification. Various other peoples regarded as distinct in Hawaii are, of course, merged under the biologically based racial stocks of Mongoloid, Caucasoid, and Negroid. But Japanese, Chinese, Filipino, Haole, Portuguese, Korean, and Puerto Rican are not racial classifications, and it is scientifically inaccurate to label a person of, let us say, part Chinese and part Japanese ancestry as racially mixed. To consider individuals of the plantation community as representing mixed cultural strains is, however, a sound and useful procedure.

Cosmopolitans thus represent a mixture of cultures; at the same time they may and commonly do represent a mixture of races. Anthropologists generally regard Hawaiians, even in "pure" form, as racially mixed, and "Hawaiians" of modern times are likely to represent recent additional mixture. Persons of part-Hawaiian ancestry often find it convenient, even when the facts of their heredity are known to them, to abbreviate their ancestry. To declare oneself "Hawaiian-Haole-Portuguese-Chinese," a combination which is not rare in Hawaii, is time-consuming, awkward to fit into employment and other records, and may be a little embarrassing in certain social contexts. It is easier to label oneself part Hawaiian or Hawaiian-Caucasian and forget the rest.

Filipinos follow a similar custom, perhaps in part because of feelings of nationalism. Nearly every adult regarded by others as being Filipino so declares himself on official records and in casual conversation. If questioned directly on this point, however, many Filipinos tell of a Spanish grandfather or great-grandfather, and the traces of Spain are evident here and there in the physical features of the Filipino population.

A few people deliberately conceal ancestry in which they have no pride, especially if their physical features allow them to do so. Puerto Rican ancestry is perhaps most likely to be treated in this fashion because it suggests a Negroid genetic background and because the social status of Puerto Ricans as a group is very low in Hawaii. A few persons identify themselves as Filipino-Spanish, whereas others regard them as Filipino–Puerto Rican.

Racial mixture is probably much greater than might be inferred from the classifications used here. But our concern is not with race, a study properly pursued by human geneticists; our categories are cultural classifications. Assignment to one or another category has depended upon the declaration of the persons concerned, and thus may represent a fair number of deliberate inaccuracies as well as an ignorance of heredity. In the main, however, the classifications are clear and meaningful if they are regarded as cultural groups. Certainly they convey much meaning to the people of the community.

Mixture of peoples is sometimes so great as to present mechanical difficulties in description. It is possible to arrive at a tremendous number of classifications if one uses all the known combinations of ancestral nationality that are recognized in Hawaii. Interethnic mixture had grown to such complexity by 1940 that Hawaiian census officials were driven to some means of simplification. Their solution was to adopt arbitrary "racial" classifications of individuals of mixed backgrounds. All persons of part-Hawaiian ancestry were lumped under the heading "part Hawaiian" regardless of other elements in their makeup. Persons of mixed Caucasian and non-Caucasian ancestry (excluding Hawaiian) were classified as "mixed" under the heading of the non-Caucasian parent, and offspring of parents neither Caucasian nor Hawaiian were classified with the father (e.g., the child of a Filipino father and a Japanese mother is "Filipino, mixed").

For the sake of simplicity, in the tables and discussion which follow all persons whose ancestry includes some Hawaiian but no Filipino genetic elements are called "part Hawaiian." Most adults placed in the part-Hawaiian group declare themselves to be "one-quarter" or more Hawaiian. I have set aside "part Filipino" as a separate class because this mixture is the most important in the community in the sense of being the most common. All persons whose ancestors include any Filipinos have been placed under this heading. Most of them have one "pure" Filipino parent, the father; nearly all the others in this category describe themselves or are described as "one-quarter" Filipino. For reference, a third classification is added for persons whose ancestry includes both Hawaiian and Filipino. To indicate the varieties and frequencies of mixtures, additional data are provided on the ancestry of children, who comprise most of the mixed population.

Cosmopolitans in the employ of the plantation total only twenty-eight persons, a very small number compared with the ratio of nearly one Cosmopolitan to four non-Cosmopolitans in the total Hawaiian population. These figures are not, however, unusual for pineapple plantations. As is common in Indonesia, continental Asia, and other parts of the world, adults of mixed descent in Hawaii are found chiefly in the larger centers of population.

Only seven adult male Cosmopolitans reside in the community of Maunaloa. Adult female Cosmopolitans total twenty-four, and the remainder of the total of 134 mixed persons are children, most of whom are the issue of mixed marriages among "pure" adults.

As might be expected from the composition of plantation personnel, by far the most important element entering into the local mixtures is Filipino. Of next greatest importance is Hawaiian, chiefly part-Hawaiian females. There are very few Chinese in the community, but they comprise the third largest component of the Cosmopolitan population. This circumstance is the result of intermarriage, in times gone by, of Hawaiian and Chinese, and the Chinese element, quantitatively small despite high frequency, comes chiefly from the same source as the Hawaiian—the part-Hawaiian wives of Filipino men. The Haole contribution is probably greater than the recorded statistics indicate, for the Hawaiian and part-Hawaiian women are likely to have some unknown and thus undeclared Haole ancestry.

Every one among the mixed population who was questioned on this matter stated that marriage with one's own people is preferable. Mixed marriages are nevertheless common, and have tended to become increasingly so as the years have passed and the number of Cosmopolitans in Hawaii has grown. There are sixty-three mixed marriages among

TABLE 6

COSMOPOLITANS OF MAUNALOA

	Adults			Children under 18	Total
	Male	Female	Total		
Part Hawaiian (no Filipino)	4	16	20	4	24
Part Filipino (incl. part Hawaiian)	3	8	11	99	110
Hawaiian-Filipino and Hawaiian-Filipino-other included in figures above	(3)	(5)	(8)	(60)	(68)
Other (no Filipino and no Hawaiian) ..	—	—	—	—	—
Total	7	24	31	103 [a]	134

[a] Many children are the offspring of Cosmopolitan marriages; that is, parents themselves are unmixed.

TABLE 7

PARENTAGE OF COSMOPOLITAN CHILDREN

	Fathers	Mothers
Filipino	85	5
Portuguese	3	6
Haole	1	6
Puerto Rican	—	6
Hawaiian	—	4
Japanese	—	4
Part Hawaiian (no Filipino)	3	29
Part Filipino (no Hawaiian)	5	18
Filipino-Hawaiian and Filipino-Hawaiian-other	5	25
Unknown	1	—
Total	103	103

TABLE 8

FREQUENCY OF NATIONALITIES IN ANCESTRY
OF COSMOPOLITAN CHILDREN [a]

Filipino	99
Hawaiian	64
Chinese	43
Puerto Rican	26
Haole	14
Portuguese	13
Japanese	10

[a] Figures represent only the frequency of incidence of ancestry and do not express genetic proportions; e.g., a total of 64 children are in varying part Hawaiian.

Maunaloa plantation employees. A large percentage of the total is, however, accounted for by Hawaiian and part-Hawaiian homesteaders, who live outside the community. Thirty-four married couples living in Maunaloa are Cosmopolitan unions. In addition to Hawaiian and Filipino, these marriages include all the recognized ethnic groups of Hawaii except Koreans—one of the groups quickest to leave the plantations and never great in number (see table 9).

Cosmopolitan adults have no social unity except so far as individuals among them might feel slight bonds through sharing a degree of common ancestry. No one in the community regards Cosmopolitans as a separate entity and they do not so regard themselves. The term "Cosmopolitan" is not used in the community and is probably meaningless to most residents. They refer to mixtures as part Hawaiian, Filipino–Puerto Rican, and so on.

As individuals, some Cosmopolitans enter actively into community affairs; as a group they have no social existence. The same statements apply to Cosmopolitan couples. Most Cosmopolitan individuals and Cosmopolitan couples are regarded, and generally regard themselves, as members of the Filipino community. Whether Hawaiian, part Hawaiian, Haole, Puerto Rican, or Japanese, a woman with a Filipino husband is ordinarily identified socially as Filipino. The Haole or Japanese wife of a Filipino is socially divorced from Haole or Japanese circles. Hawaiian and part-Hawaiian women may, however, have many social ties with relatives outside the community who are not Filipino.

For most Cosmopolitans and for wives of Filipinos, social identification and affiliation with the Filipinos seem to present no real problems.
These persons are referred to individually as Hawaiian (the term used
for anyone who has discernible Hawaiian physical traits), Haole, and
so on, but their social lives are with and as Filipinos, among whom they
are well received.

The few Cosmopolitan couples of which neither spouse is Filipino
set themselves apart from Filipinos, and are often set apart also by holding plantation positions of high status. A few part Filipinos set themselves apart in similar manner. Declaration of "nationality" among
persons partly or largely of Filipino ancestry is sometimes an index of
social distinction. The rare individual who identifies himself on official
records as "Filipino-Spanish" usually regards himself as culturally
distinct from members of the Filipino community and is in fact culturally distinct in the attitudes he holds and the customs he observes.

For Cosmopolitan couples who are not socially identified as part of
the Filipino community, adjustment to plantation community life may
be trying. Their social contacts may be limited almost entirely to those
of the working day and to their relatives in the community or on the
island. A few who have entered mixed marriages have felt themselves
stigmatized—more so than the attitudes of others in the community
might warrant—and suffer unhappiness on this account. The reaction
of a few such persons has been to turn against the group of their original
affiliation. Still others (and the total number of the Cosmopolitans and
Cosmopolitan couples not identified with the Filipino community is
small), although closely identified with no group, appear to lead happy
and active social lives in association with more than one group in the
community.

If the social assignment of husband and wife as determined by education, income, and familial background is nearly equal, a Cosmopolitan
couple may fit fairly well into the social structure, associating with one
of the strata of the community. If there are marked differences between
husband and wife in these respects, the couple is likely to become an
anomaly, and finds no social identification. The wife who feels socially
degraded by placement with her husband's group may suffer, for she
can ordinarily have no other assignment. Such women are few.

Most of the Cosmopolitan marriages are between Filipino men and
part-Hawaiian women or other women of social status never very much

Family group, three generations, right to left: Filipino grandfather; Filipino–Puerto Rican–Hawaiian daughter; grandchildren (father, Filipino).

At the beach, summer educational program. Foreground, left to right: Puerto Rican, Haole, Japanese, Filipino.

Newly planted fields with mulch paper between the rows.

Planting. Disked-down plants serve to retain moisture.

Mechanical harvester.

Mechanical harvester showing conveyor belt.

Houses in Filipino Camp.

A house on "The Hill."

higher than that of their husbands. A number of such marriages have ended in divorce, but most of them seem to be enduring. Part-Hawaiian and Hawaiian wives frequently express the view that they are fortunate in marrying Filipinos. Filipino men, they state, make highly desirable husbands, treating their wives with kindness and consideration, giving them as much money to spend as incomes will allow, and at the same time demanding of them little hard work.

TABLE 9

COSMOPOLITAN UNIONS

Husbands		Wives									
		Fil.	Chin.	Haole	Port.	P. Rican	Japan.	Haw.	Pt. Haw.	Pt. Fil.	Haw.-Fil. and Haw.-Fil.-other
Filipino	22			1	2	2	1	2	10	4	(2)
Chinese	3			1			1		1		
Haole	1								1		
Portuguese .	1								1		
Japanese ...	—										
Hawaiian ..	—										
Puerto Rican											
Part Hawaiian (no Filipino)	4	1							1	2	(1)
Part Filipino (inc. Hawaiian)	3	2		1							
Hawaiian-Filipino and Hawaiian-Filipino-other	(1)									(1)	
Total	34	3		3	2	2	2	2	14	6	(3)

The young children of Cosmopolitan couples appear to suffer no distress in adjusting to the community. Problems attributable to mixed racial and cultural background lie in the future. Approximately one-third of the children of the community are Cosmopolitans; hence they are not a minority but the second largest group of children in the community. Most of them are of part-Filipino background and mingle intimately with "pure" Filipino children, the largest single group of children. Filipino and part-Filipino children are seldom distinguished, and certainly the children themselves make few distinctions. Considerations of this kind do not seem to enter the consciousness of children until they approach maturity, and, judging from the histories of mixed children who have matured in the community, solid placement in the Filipino community is a matter of course for most of them.

The problem of adjustment of Cosmopolitans will, in all probability, continue to dwindle in magnitude as their number increases and as cultural differences derived from their ancestors disappear.

VII | *Community Social Relationships*

In this discussion of the people of Maunaloa, the subjects of social distinctions and social relationships have been touched upon many times. The cultural factors which set one group above another group and some individuals above others within those groups are numerous. All are familiar in other communities of the United States and of the world. The combination of circumstances within Maunaloa may, however, be said to be unique in the sense that it is peculiar to Hawaii, deriving, on the one hand, from the nature of the community as a company town, and, on the other hand, from historic circumstances of the mingling of cultures in Hawaii.

A general statement of social classifications recognized within the community is as follows: at the social peak is a small group of Haoles; next in rank is a considerably larger group of persons of Japanese ancestry; at the bottom is a large group of Filipinos, their spouses, and other persons of varying and often mixed ancestry. A scattering of the socially peripheral runs through this hierarchy rather like nuts in a layer cake, compatible with the cake but easily distinguishable. This formulation cannot be compared with a classification of Hawaii as a whole because some racial-cultural groups of the Territory are absent or nearly absent from Maunaloa.

Social rank within the three major strata at Maunaloa is determined almost wholly by occupation. The principal exception is the intra-Japanese social stigma attached to Okinawan birth or parentage. Intra-Filipino social distinctions by Philippine cultural group are not truly hierarchical. Ilocanos, for example, are not socially inferior to Visayans.

This simplified statement of social stratification may suggest arrangement principally or solely on the basis of "race." But such an interpretation would be inaccurate. The social scheme is based upon two major factors: one's job on the plantation and one's racial-cultural affiliation or that of his ancestors. Occupational rank seems to be the more important of the two criteria, but they cut across each other in so many and diverse ways that neither may be said to dominate the other.

In Hawaii, so-called "race" has always been much more a cultural than a biological consideration, as witness the classifications Haole, Portuguese, Spanish, and Puerto Rican. Moreover, Haoles do not occupy their position only because they are genetically Haoles; Japanese do not hold their assignment because of anything inherent in Japanese ancestry; and Filipinos are not accorded their place in the hierarchy solely on the grounds of being Filipinos.

The term "Haole" clearly implies that individuals so designated meet the cultural criteria of Haole-hood and that they are Caucasians of any European derivation except Portuguese and Spanish. (There are no persons identified as Spanish in the Maunaloa population.) Given genetic Haole status, the most important additional qualification is occupational. The male Haole should have a good salaried position or, if young and relatively new in the employment of the corporation, the promise of such a position. A Haole should have a spouse who is a Haole, speech free of any trace of Pidgin English, and he should avoid intimate social relations with most non-Haoles.

The Haole may be deficient in one or another of these qualifications. His job need not carry a high rating, for example, but it cannot be very low. The genetic Haole who is paid by the hour is at a great social disadvantage, and a man regularly employed as a field laborer is hardly considered a Haole.

The Haole who habitually and intimately associates with non-Haoles jeopardizes his own status, since their social standing may be inferior. Cases at point are the few genetically Haole women who are wives of Filipinos. Hardly acquainted with the socially Haole women of the community, their ties are with "the Filipino camp," and their inclusion in the Haole group is unthinkable, even if education and prior social background otherwise qualified them for admission. Another example is the lone male genetic Haole among employees paid by the hour. Holding a minor salaried position at the time of his first employment but lacking formal education and social polish, he was then on the fringe of the Haole circle. With demotion to a lower and hourly-paid job and adoption of a habit of off-work association with Filipino men, his social placement is with the Filipinos. He is automatically excluded from Haole social gatherings and reference to "Haoles" ordinarily omits him. A Haole college boy who works during the summer as field laborer remains unquestionably Haole, however, and is regarded with respect for his industry.

The fact that the title "Haole" has cultural as well as genetic requirements is sometimes clearly expressed by island residents. A part-Hawaiian resident of Kaunakakai, for example, denied that the several Haoles of Maunaloa who are socially identified with Filipinos had Haole status. In discussing the number of Haoles in the plantation community, he summarily dismissed these persons with an idiosyncratic but clearly comprehensible term: "Oh, those local Haoles! We have a few of them here, too."

A Portuguese man holding a good salaried position stands socially distinct. His status is fairly good, but there are very few Portuguese in the community, and he fits in with no other group. Given a college education, poise in social contacts with Haoles, and speech, interests, and attitudes which conform to the Haole standard, he might become socially identified with the Haole group. In the history of Maunaloa, where Portuguese have always been few, no person has done this, and it is probably extremely uncommon in any Hawaiian plantation community. The social placement of Portuguese hourly employees of the plantation and of Portuguese wives of hourly employees is unmistakably low. The few who meet this description have Filipino or Cosmopolitan spouses and are identified with the Filipino camp.

The Japanese middle class consists of several groupings: nisei holding good supervisory positions, nisei employed as skilled or semiskilled hourly workmen, issei from Honshu or Kyushu, and issei from Okinawa. With a single exception these categories are loosely formed. Only the nisei who hold supervisory positions form an in-group whose members customarily associate with one another as intimates. This small group may associate also with the few non-Haoles of similar occupational rank. Social attributes of these nisei are predominantly, and frequently consciously, American middle-class customs and attitudes. Membership in the golf club is an important symbol of social status to men and to some women. Nisei are careful, also, to speak "good" English.

An important mark of social elevation to the nisei (and other non-

Haole) wives of plantation supervisors is membership in an ethnically mixed bridge club composed only of wives of supervisory employees. Meetings are held in the homes of members, and participation is by invitation only. Invitation is initiated, along the lines of plantation employment, by the senior women, who are wives of Haole supervisors. The geographical and thus the social area of one's residence determines membership in the bridge club. By custom, an arbitrary line on membership disqualifies any woman whose home is in the camps.

As a mixed group on a fairly intimate level of interpersonal relationships, this bridge club is both unusual and socially important. Only a few years old, it represents circumstances once regarded as impossible. Even if Haole women had been receptive to a mixed bridge club in the early days, there would not have been enough non-Haole women who might be suitable as members. Thanks in large measure to this bridge club, relationships between Haole and nisei women have in recent years become closer and the social breach between them has narrowed. No counterpart exists among men, perhaps because they have less interest in bridge.

Intra-Japanese social distinctions among hourly-employed nisei and among issei are on an individual basis. The social status of issei, although inferior to that of the nisei elite, is by no means low. Rather, they stand apart as having little social identity. The Okinawa-born rate low socially. Whatever the individual rating of issei or nisei, they are set rather sharply apart from the Haoles above them and from the Filipino community below them.

Social distinctions among Filipinos are complex, involving not only social distances between Philippine linguistic and subcultural groups but also occupationally based distinctions. Only status conferred by rank in plantation employment is important, however, in hierarchical social placement. *Lunas* and their families form a raggedly defined ingroup of the highest social prestige. Below them are the men employed by the hour, among whom many small and socially separate groups exist. Resting on propinquity, common interests, and personal likes and dislikes, these unstable groups are hardly recognized as entities and are not hierarchically arranged. Individual social placement among hourly-employed Filipinos depends upon their jobs and also their personal qualities. Single men are regarded as outside the social scheme.

Cosmopolitans may find social placement anywhere on the scale from the bottom to a peak of marginal affiliation with the Haoles. Assignment depends primarily upon the occupational status of the male and upon such matters as education and poise in social relationships with Haoles. The genetically Hawaiian-Haole may be socially acceptable if he is the cultural equal or superior of genetically Haole individuals in job, education, and social background of parents, and if he conducts himself as a social equal. As in Hawaii at large, part Hawaiians (and also Hawaiians) may have high social status provided they also have economic prestige, education, and social graces. In the history of Maunaloa, however, no individual of part-Hawaiian ancestry has been fully assimilated as a member of the topmost social group. Factors which have created this feeling of apartness seem to be a combination of mild "racial" prejudice and the failure of the individual to meet the cultural requirements for full acceptance.

Physical appearance sometimes enters into social placement of Cosmopolitans, as it does wherever physically and culturally different peoples have come together and racial prejudice has arisen. Although the term "passing" is not customary in Hawaii, passing in the sense that some undesirable elements in one's genetic background may be concealed is not unusual. The impetus to "pass" is not nearly so great as in the continental United States. The breach between Caucasian and non-Caucasian in Hawaii is very much less than that between Caucasian and Negro in the continental United States. Hawaiian Cosmopolitans, although not united, comprise a majority rather than a minority group, and discriminatory attitudes in Hawaii have never been extreme. Even among persons who openly and proudly declare their Cosmopolitan ancestry, however, it is an advantage to look like a Haole.

As ununited minorities, Cosmopolitans, Cosmopolitan couples, and Portuguese who have good occupational ratings stand fairly well apart from any social grouping. Similar circumstances apply to the few Chinese. Holding good if not the best positions, they find their closest identification with the socially highest placed of the Japanese, with whom they associate most frequently, but seldom on an intimate, familial basis.

We have scarcely mentioned Puerto Ricans in this account because they are so few at Maunaloa and do not form a group. Throughout the

Territory their social status is extremely low, below that of Filipinos. As individuals at Maunaloa their status is equally low, although they tend to be socially identified with the Filipinos.

Within the community of Maunaloa, inherited membership in a racial-cultural group places upward but not downward limits on social mobility. We have seen that a genetic Haole may be socially placed anywhere from top to bottom. The range of a Japanese, Chinese, Portuguese, or part Hawaiian has a lower topmost limit. Puerto Ricans, Filipinos, and part Filipinos have the least potential mobility, but the range within the lowest stratum is fairly great. Within the limits stated, placement on the social scale depends almost entirely upon occupational status. Plantation positions of equal salary and prestige are held by Haoles, Japanese, Chinese, Portuguese, and part Hawaiians. (No Filipino has yet held a supervisory position of high prestige.) The social affiliation of an individual, however, is limited by his birth. A Haole of lower occupational rating than, let us say, a Japanese or Chinese will nevertheless have higher social standing than they.

Opportunities for occupational mobility are fairly great, but for non-Haoles the upward path ends before the heights are reached. Supervisory and administrative positions on the plantation have depended upon education and training, and in the past few persons except Haoles have been eligible. With the passage of years a growing number of non-Haoles have become technically qualified for positions of authority, and hold them. The occupational peaks, however, remain beyond the reach of any except Haoles.

Non-Haoles lack social experience and poise in dealing with Haoles. This is a matter not to be lightly dismissed. For peoples conditioned by a lifetime of social assignment inferior to that of Haoles, assurance in dealing with Haoles as equals is not easily come by. Attitudes of superiority among Haoles in subsidiary positions might also disrupt a smooth chain of command and thus hamper plantation operations.

The second deficiency stems from the influence of attitudes held in the continental United States. A non-Haole who might in technical knowledge and experience as well as social presence meet all requirements for a top plantation position could nevertheless not reach this height. A plantation official, especially of a mainland-financed corporation, comes into contact with both local and mainland business executives. Particularly in relations with men from the continental United States, it is considered undesirable to have anyone except a member of the Caucasoid race serve as the agent.

It must be added that present-day officials of the plantation personally express little ethnocentrism, but they are well aware of the attitudes within their own community and abroad. They themselves feel that Hawaii and still more the mainland are "not ready" for high-ranking officials of any race but Caucasian.

Filipinos and persons identified with them as part of the "Filipino camp" find upward social movement the most difficult. Even if a Filipino had great ability and the requisite education and social graces, he would nevertheless find occupational ascent and concomitant social rise restricted. It is most unlikely that a Filipino having these accomplishments would even seek plantation employment. Filipinos are not denied all opportunity to hold good positions. A substantial number have supervisory positions, but their authority is almost always over persons who are also Filipinos. No Filipino holds a position which ranks high in the occupational hierarchy, but at the same time probably no person qualified for such a position in every respect except his Filipino descent has been passed over.

According to plantation officials, the local and outside worlds are not yet ready to accept Filipinos in positions of authority, and Filipinos themselves are not prepared to assume such positions. Non-Filipinos of the community, for the most part, appear not to begrudge better jobs to Filipinos, but feel that a Filipino must possess all the qualifications in ample measure.

The influence of ethnic affiliations may be stated in another way. If two aspirants, one Japanese and one Haole, are equally qualified for a good position on the plantation (except, of course, for their racial background), the Haole will almost surely be given the post. If the Japanese has superior qualifications, he might win the position. Of two equally qualified candidates, one Japanese and one Filipino, the Japanese will almost certainly be favored unless the position is one of authority over Filipinos. With two equally qualified candidates, one Haole and one Filipino, there is not the slightest doubt that the Haole will be chosen.

Although hierarchical distinctions within the three major social classifications are based chiefly on occupational rank, inherited status and personal attributes of both males and females may enhance or depreciate their positions. The social status of women, as we have noted, corresponds closely with that of their husbands, regardless of the premium which birth into a socially favored ethnic group might otherwise confer. Within the group of their social assignment, however, ascribed status gives women some prestige. Filipino and other non-Haole women of the Filipino camp regard the few Haole wives of Filipino men as being "rather special" because they are genetically Haole. A reputation for being intelligent, virtuous, or industrious also gives prestige, although it does not alter assignment to social strata.

In only one ethnic and social group, however, do women enter importantly as determinants of the social status of themselves, their husbands, and their children. Among the Haoles the attributes of wives affect the careers of their husbands. As in the higher echelons of employment in urban corporations, the personal qualities of a plantation official's wife are important. A "good" wife, one who wins the regard of others, helps to make her husband an acceptable candidate for advancement. A "bad" wife who is disliked by others and causes discord is detrimental to her husband's career. It is only for higher-ranking positions that the qualities of an employee's wife are actively considered when his promotion is at stake. Among hourly employees and personnel in minor supervisory positions, the personal attributes of wives are of no concern unless the wives cause serious trouble in the community.

Differentials in occupational status and the social distinctions they entail serve not only to discourage unity by ethnic group but also to weaken ties of kinship. This is, of course, a commonplace in the continental United States. The circumstances are noteworthy for Hawaii, however, because they are in sharp contrast to kin relationships among the social classes of Japan and the Philippines from which Hawaiian plantation labor was drawn. In rural Japan and the Philippines, wellbeing and survival depend largely upon one's relatives. Ties of kinship are correspondingly close and entail many reciprocal privileges and obligations. At Maunaloa plantation the employment of close relatives is frowned upon unless the relatives are in positions of no authority. A moderate number of close relatives are included, however, among community members, chiefly the dependents of employees. If the occupational status of the heads of related families is markedly different, social contacts among even the closest kin in these families may be inhibited. Concrete examples are several sisters in the community whose husbands' positions differ greatly in salary and social prestige. These women may visit each other informally and participate in affairs such as marriages and funerals of the families of their birth, but their social identifications and, increasingly as time passes, their important social affiliations follow the social assignments of their husbands.

Insignia of social rank which convey meaning to all members of the community are various. Most important of these is the location of one's house. Residence on "The Hill" is the symbol of highest premium. To move from camp to the periphery of "The Hill," as some nisei and other non-Haole families have done, is an important upward social step. Social altitude is correlated with physical elevation; the best houses are high on the hill, and the Filipino camp is on the lowest level.

A plantation employee may have supervisory status but not receive the full social standing to which it might entitle him and his family unless he resides in the appropriate area, a circumstance which has occasionally arisen when men residing in camp have been promoted but suitable housing in the supervisory area has not been available.

Among Haoles—perhaps because they are few in number—other distinctive patterns of behavior and insignia of social status consist principally of traits which are common to middle-class American whites elsewhere in the United States. The material possessions of Haoles are generally superior in cost and quality to those of other peoples of the community, but they are less likely to attribute importance to such things as the ownership of a new car or a television set. Perhaps because they feel immune to censure in this respect, and, more importantly, because it is easier and cheaper, Haole women tend to be less careful of their clothing and grooming than other young women of the community while engaged in the ordinary affairs of the day. One of the traditional activities of middle-class American life, the playing of golf, seems to have been left almost entirely to the nisei. Although Haoles took the initiative in the formation of the local golf clubs, they seem to have lost interest in the game.

There is considerable emulation of the Haoles among other peoples of the community. This pattern is most noticeable among non-Haole supervisors in positions of authority, and is not surprising in view of the fact that the plantation is an ingrown community of employees, most of whom have received their professional training on the plantation. Non-Haole men in salaried positions have had instruction and supervision for many years from their occupational superiors, most of whom have been Haole. In addition to learning skills of the job, they have imitated their teachers in other ways.

The informal uniform and insignia of office of the manager and assistant manager has for years been a white broadcloth shirt and necktie, worn without a coat. Poorly suited to the physical environment because one trip through the plantation fields will often soil the white shirt, it nevertheless serves, even to a stranger, to distinguish its wearer as a man of authority. Down the occupational echelon of supervisors, emulation takes various forms. Colored dress shirts with neckties are favored by a few of the higher supervisors, and tieless open dress shirts are worn by others of lower rank. Employees who are paid by the hour wear clothing clearly identifiable as work clothes.

When "the boss" changed from high-topped field boots to low shoes, field boots soon virtually disappeared from the plantation scene. When he changed one brand of whisky for another, the storekeeper noted a sharp decline and a concomitant rise in sales of the two whiskies.

Emulation sometimes goes far beyond material objects. Repetitions of the sentiments of the manager delivered with his characteristic vocabulary and turns of expression if with island phonemes are not uncommon. Gestures and other mannerisms are adopted also.

On the job, interpersonal relationships follow the occupational hierarchy closely, as it is felt that they must in order to ensure efficient operation of the plantation; racial affiliation or nonoccupational status is essentially—at least overtly— disregarded. The working day of most persons except field laborers brings them into frequent and direct contact with other employees of differing cultural backgrounds and social status. The overt atmosphere is one of coöperation and amiability. Covert tensions and hostilities unquestionably exist, but the working day is not the time to express them.

As in other industries, a workman might see his supervisor daily for years but know virtually nothing about him. He may, however, derive much secondhand and often inaccurate knowledge of his superiors from gossip. Most supervisors have little interest in the rank and file of workmen. Residence in a common and small area, however, encourages awareness of the affairs of others, and certain supervisors take both professional and personal interest in the lives of underlings close to them.

Working orders are usually given in the form of directions. Many Haole supervisors have adopted, independently or by emulation of older employees, patterns of joking relationship with men under them. These patterns are particularly useful when the occupational breach is great. Jocose reciprocity is the most frequent response, but both parties understand that the jocularity does not deny authority or seriousness.

With one's equals, near-equals, and inferiors the standard terms of address are personal names, nicknames, diminutives, or surnames unadorned by honorific prefixes. Superiors are ordinarily addressed by their surname with the prefix "Mr." Overlying all social intercourse at work, even among persons representing the greatest extremes in status, is an atmosphere of informality as compared with mainland business concerns.

Social relationship among persons of different class does not end with the working day, but the permissible and proper occasions for it are clearly limited. Intermingling occurs in community-wide social gatherings: the annual carnival to raise funds for other community affairs, events of the school calendar, Boy Scout and Girl Scout programs, university extension lectures for women, and the Christmas program for children.

Athletic events, baseball, basketball, volleyball, and, theoretically at least, golf, are other occasions for social mixing. Athletic teams cross all racial and cultural borders. The members of these teams are on informal and friendly if not intimate terms. A community fishing club for men, in existence chiefly because it allows members to fish in otherwise forbidden waters, crosses social barriers. Most of the members are Filipinos and Japanese, but anyone may participate with full social approval of the community.

Supervisory employees have a greater number of approved occasions for social mixing with persons of different social status and racial-cultural background. The annual party of supervisory employees, quite like the "office party," golf tournaments, picnics, and meetings of the women's bridge club are all approved occasions for crossing old "racial" lines. Social distinctions, particularly those based upon one's job, are, however, clearly preserved upon these occasions.

Friendliness and mutual respect exist in these relationships which cross social and racial lines, but intimacy is discouraged. Plantation officials explicitly declare that a moderate degree of formality and segregation in accordance with the occupational hierarchy is desirable for the efficient prosecution of plantation affairs. This policy is extended along the line of command in work rather than referring to social distinctions based upon race or cultural background. The Filipino foreman, for example, is discouraged from intimate association with the men under him. If, as sometimes happens, a Filipino foreman takes up residence with some of the men under him, he is urged to hold himself apart.

Perhaps many are willing to mingle with social superiors, but few desire to be intimate with their inferiors. This attitude is, of course, not merely an indication of social snobbery. Intimacy requires similarity in interests and values, which one is most likely to find among his equals.

Regardless of the esteem between two socially segregated males, they do not associate on an intimate familial basis. Haoles usually invite only Haoles to intimate dinner or cocktail parties. The few non-Haoles who receive such invitations are usually spouses of Haoles, and may reside in other communities. Japanese, in similar fashion, associate intimately only with Japanese. Persons who have lived in the community from childhood tend to have a few warm friendships, established during school days, which cross social and racial lines. Despite these bonds, however, the social distinctions in the community tend to prevent intimacy.

The attitude that social distances should be preserved sometimes exists among those in the lowest social class. The rare Haole newcomer who invites Filipinos to his home may be surprised when they decline the invitation on the grounds that such socializing is not appropriate. If the invitation is accepted, as it might be by the young Hawaii-born Filipinos or part Filipinos, it rarely leads to intimate friendship for lack of sufficient common interests. Some have refused the opportunity to elevate themselves socially because it would make them feel ill at ease. Some non-Haoles are clearly never at ease in the presence of their Haole social superiors.

Racial-cultural background is an important consideration both at work and in nonprofessional social contexts. The "nationality" of the employee and his wife are very useful inclusions in personnel records. Reference to a stranger invariably includes some identification of his national background. The name alone may suffice; Japanese and Chinese names, for example, are distinctive. If the speaker does not make clear the racial-cultural classification of a third person under discussion, he is sure to be asked. Such a query by no means reflects only ethnic prejudice. It is practical information which may reveal a good deal about the person and serve as a guide in relationships with him.

Social exclusiveness along racial-cultural lines is most marked among the Haoles and the Japanese. But other considerations also enter, and it is impossible to state in quantitative terms the influence that this attitude alone exerts in keeping peoples socially apart. If one crosses social boundaries, the less the descent along the lines of social class as determined by job and cultural background as well as by racial-cultural affiliation, the less the fall from grace.

Japanese nearly always marry Japanese, although the tendency to cross racial-cultural lines in marriage is growing. Nisei express themselves as having no serious objection to out-marriage of their children, except with Puerto Ricans and Filipinos. A Japanese who marries both out and downward is socially excluded. The several male Japanese employees who have crossed racial lines do not live in the plantation community, and their social contacts with Japanese are limited almost entirely to those of the working day. (One nisei informant volunteered to "explain" the marriages of these men to non-Japanese women by stating that the men were members of old Japanese families in Hawaii— and thus presumably had had long exposure to an atmosphere of relative freedom from racial prejudice.)

Filipinos are the least exclusive of the three major groups of the community, and cultivate warm personal relations with all receptive outsiders. They express social contempt for Negroes, but there are no Negroes in the community or on the island except so far as Negroid genetic elements are included in Hawaiians, Puerto Ricans, and Filipinos themselves (a few of whom might have Negroid genetic elements as a result of admixture of their ancestors with Philippine Negritos). They favor marriage with Filipinos as the wisest choice, but have little objection to marriage with other peoples. To marry upward in the Hawaiian social scale is regarded as a coup. A Filipino feels pride in marrying a Haole or a Japanese. As one Filipino stated, "A man would feel that he put something over if he married a Japanese woman."

The lone and curious Filipino exception to freedom in intermarriage is with Japanese males. The reasons for objection are clearly not "racial," since Japanese females are not only acceptable but, from the standpoint of males at least, desirable. But Filipino girls are firm in rejecting the idea of marriage to men of Japanese extraction because they "think themselves so much better than women," "expect women to do too much for them," "are too bossy," and "aren't much fun."

For persons growing up in the community, separation into Haole, Japanese, and Filipino groups begins in childhood. Small children of any racial-cultural background may associate freely during early childhood, at play, at school, in the summer educational programs sponsored jointly by the county and the corporation, and in the Boy Scout and Girl Scout organizations. Some parents, especially the Haole and the Japanese, tend to keep their children apart from others even at this early age. There are not many Haole children, and they are geographically removed from most non-Haole children because of the location of their homes; so their intermingling may be confined to school and other community ventures for children. Girls are given less encouragement than boys to mix socially with "other races." For both boys and girls, however, a marked social separation develops before they finish grammar school, and thereafter the estrangement increases.

Despite the social distances which exist, off-work relationships are cordial. Haoles and Japanese evince mutual respect and are friendly. From long association, men feel at ease with men and, increasingly, women are at ease with women. Social contacts which cross lines of both sex and race are a different matter. Few persons, either Haole or Japanese, feel comfortable under these circumstances unless the contact is fleeting and casual.

Haole relations with people of the Filipino camp are fewer than with Japanese and, although consistently pleasant, rarely have an atmosphere of equality. Haole women may live in the community for years with no more than casual acquaintance with Filipinos. They might come into contact with Filipino women many times at P.T.A. meetings, or at camp weddings to which they and their husbands are invited. The few long-time Haole women residents who are active in community affairs may have a wide if not intimate acquaintance among women of the camp, which seldom progresses beyond the exchange of casual greetings. Social contacts of Haole women with Filipino men are almost nonexistent except in occasional patron-like attendance at Filipino weddings.

But the lack of close social relationships is by no means predicated solely on racial considerations. Given a community in the continental

United States formed around a nucleus of five hundred employees of a single concern, all of the same race, it is unlikely that the wives of company officials would know many workmen and their families. Even the officials themselves would not have this acquaintance unless the nature of their work made it necessary or useful. Because of the isolation of Maunaloa, the socially superior are, in fact, better aware of the identities of those below them than they would be in company towns on the mainland.

Off-work relationships between Japanese and Filipino, like those between Haole and Filipino, are limited to community affairs and athletics. Intimate intermingling with Filipinos is unthinkable to most Japanese. The rare Japanese who have associated freely with Filipinos have been single men, who may cross social lines with less jeopardy than women or married men, and their Filipino associates have been males.

Living for decades in closely grouped subcommunities, often in dwellings placed side by side, the Filipinos and the Japanese have, clearly at the instigation of the Japanese, maintained sharply separate social identities. Yet relations between them have been remarkably peaceful. None of the numerous long-time residents of the community queried on this subject could recall one instance of physical violence between Filipinos and Japanese, although a few intra-Japanese and many intra-Filipino quarrels are remembered. (Several managers of other plantations made the same response.) Filipinos say that they "respect" the Japanese and also the Haoles.

It is interesting to note that no clearly formed unflattering stereotype of either Japanese or Haole appears to exist in Maunaloa. Haoles may sometimes refer to Japanese in half-joking terms as "inscrutable" (much more likely to be expressed as "You never know what they're thinking"). The customary references, however, are of praise, referring to efficiency, faithfulness, and dependability.

For Hawaiians, Portuguese, Puerto Ricans, and Filipinos, however, unflattering stereotypes are commonly expressed, as they are elsewhere in Hawaii. The "Portagee" is said to be vulgar, loud-mouthed, and stupid. The Puerto Rican ("Borinki"—a highly derogatory term, perhaps derived from the rendition of the name Puerto Rican in one of the Philippine dialects) is "at the bottom of the human trash pile," inferior in every respect. The Hawaiian (Kanaka) is gay, charming, and carefree, but he is also lazy, careless, a poor provider, and unreliable.

The Filipinos, for whom no term of opprobrium is in common use, may be described as gay and carefree, but, according to other peoples of Maunaloa, they have many undesirable traits: Filipinos are "lazy," "act just like children," "live for today," "think only of pleasure," "have no sense of morals," "will do anything," "will eat anything, even dogs," "just got out of the trees," "are emotionally unreliable," and "may turn on one at any moment." They "can't get along even among themselves," "won't accept responsibility," and "are not community-minded."

Ethnocentrism of this kind is roughly correlated with occupational status. The higher one's job on the plantation, the less marked these attitudes and the less the tendency to ascribe to race such cultural attributes as moral standards.

Filipinos are well aware of these sentiments and, though they maintain good relations with other peoples, are resentful. Many feel that they are discriminated against, both at work and in community affairs, and are eager to express themselves on the subject to the sympathetic listener: "Japanese and Haoles get the best jobs." "If two truck drivers get into a crackup—one's a Filipino and one's a Japanese—the Filipino is always to blame." "Filipinos don't get their share of community funds." "We'd take a bigger part in community affairs if they'd let us." (Office in the community council, the most important organization, is by election, and potential Filipino voters far outnumber all others.)

Dissatisfaction with plantation work and community life extends far beyond charges of discrimination. Wages are too low, rents too high, houses inadequately maintained, and recreational facilities limited. The actual number of malcontents is probably few, but their voices are loud. These complaints seem in part to represent defense reactions against the low esteem in which Filipinos are held in Hawaii. They also constitute a means of venting hostility derived from this and other sources. Besides the tensions arising from feelings of social debasement, many Filipinos are insecure about their jobs in the face of increasing mechanization and dwindling needs for labor. Some Filipinos, as well as other people of the same social status, are afraid of their superiors at first. A new Haole supervisor is a potential menace ("make me scare like hell") until he is proved harmless.

The insecurity and hostility of members of the Filipino community are not expressed in the form of aggressive behavior toward Japanese or Haoles. A few persons have sought comfort in religion. The small success of religious sects which offer salvation has been among Filipinos and other members of the Filipino community, but Filipinos of good position and relatively high social standing are not included among the converts.

Of importance as a butt of aggression is a vaguely conceived bugaboo called "the company," which is held responsible for everything bad—not only occupational and domestic ills but also social difficulties. Some Filipinos believe that it is the company which prevents the Japanese from having free social intercourse with Filipinos and also prevents all other intergroup social mingling.

Closely allied with the evils laid at the door of the company are those arising from racial prejudice, to which Filipinos tend to impute greater importance than circumstances would seem to warrant. Ignoring considerations of education, experience, and ability, many express the belief that their lowly occupational status rests entirely upon the fact that they are Filipinos. As some individuals put their case, "A Filipino hasn't got a chance."

Objectification of the company varies. To some it is personified by the personnel manager and the highest plantation officers. To others—perhaps to most—the company means none of these persons because even the topmost officials are manifestly employees who work for compensation just as the Filipinos themselves do. The locus as well as the form of the company is usually indefinite.

Staunchly allied with the Filipinos in its attitude toward the company is the union, which is the chief agency for effective offense and defense. Points at issue in union demands throughout the years have often been of genuine importance to the welfare of plantation employees. However, grievances have arisen over the most trivial issues. Occasionally the union has even presented demands (instigated, of course, by representatives in the employ of the plantation) that were actually opposed to the wishes of the employees concerned.

As an essentially mythical entity, "the company" serves as a useful scapegoat. By diverting aggression against other groups into less harmful channels, it aids in preserving the manifest harmony which characterizes intergroup and interclass relations and which is necessary for successful operation of the plantation.

VIII | *Technological and Social Change*

When Maunaloa plantation began operations in the early 1920's, a handful of supervisory employees directed a large body of illiterate laborers. Domestic facilities for workmen were crude, wooden-based tents housing groups of men, and communal messes, baths, and toilets. The few supervisory employees lived in more substantial wooden dwellings. Motor vehicles were few and roads were poor.

Lacking suitable means of transport for the many large crews of men then necessary, the management followed the usual procedure for the plantations of Hawaii, and placed groups of dwellings among the pineapple fields within walking distance of work. Three separate clusters of dwellings were erected over a distance of several miles on the slopes of Mauna Loa. These settlements were called camps.

No official policy of segregation by race existed, although one community tended from the beginning toward a Filipino population. After a few years, when housing for married men and their families became available, Japanese families were more heavily concentrated in another community.

Few official records regarding the personnel of the first decade of the plantation's existence have been retained, but old employees give a clear if general picture of the conditions of life and the nature of plantation personnel. Field workmen included gangs of aging Korean and Chinese employees. These men disappeared from the plantation by the early 1930's. Most employees were Filipinos, nearly all of whom were single or had left their families behind in the Philippines.

After housing for families and educational facilities for children were made available, Japanese employees with families increased in number. There were extremely few Hawaiian and part-Hawaiian employees until 1927, when the fields of the Hoolehua homesteads were brought under cultivation, and the homesteaders, who continued to live in their homestead dwellings, were hired. Living quarters for Filipinos and other non-Hawaiian employees working in the Hoolehua fields were erected in that area.

In the frontier-like atmosphere of the first decade of the plantation's existence, Filipinos, and sometimes also other peoples, carried weapons for both offense and defense. So uncommon today as to be objects of curiosity, these were small dagger-like knives in sheaths, sometimes shaped like fountain pens for concealment and convenience in carrying. Physical violence among the workmen was common, and the communities were under the surveillance of the "camp police," employed by the plantation.

Some roughness also characterized relationships between employee and boss. Physical violence directed toward inferiors, always officially disapproved, was rare, but vehement verbal censure was common. A manager could hire, fire, punish, and reward according to his whims, and employees had no means of appeal.

Virtually confined to their small camps by lack of roads and public transportation, workmen had few amusements. The trip of nearly twenty miles to the principal town was hardly a pleasurable adventure through the clouds of red dust on the narrow dirt road, and, when one reached his destination, he found uncomfortable heat and little to do which could not be done in greater comfort at home. The principal diversions of field workers were gambling and drinking. On paydays a troop of prostitutes would visit the camps for a day or two with the sanction of the management. But, as with most other aspects of life, even relationships with these women were superintended. Examined for venereal disease by the company physician before they began to serve their clientele, the women were instructed when to enter the community and when to leave it.

A heavy stamp of paternalism, not always kindly, characterized relations between supervisors and workmen. Each camp had in residence a supervisory employee who filled the roles of patron, arbitrator, and watchdog. Aided by the camp police, he kept order in the small community and dispensed justice. If he were a little heavy-handed and quixotic in this last capacity, those were his privileges.

Operation of the plantation depended upon the muscles of men, aided by simple hand tools, and mules to pull plows, harrows, and cultivators. Fruit and supplies were transported by truck to and from the plantation port, a few miles from the borders of the pineapple fields. On the plantation, supervisors usually rode horseback and other employees walked.

The plantation has tended steadily toward increased mechanization. Well before 1930, field employees who had to travel long distances were transported by truck, and tractors had begun to displace the mule teams. By the early 1930's, few persons walked to work. As horses and mules grew too old for labor they were replaced by machines. The last team of mules, long used only for digging drainage ditches and for cultivating oddly shaped corners poorly suited to the use of tractors, was retired in 1937. The last saddle horse, retired from active service for several years and kept chiefly for sentimental reasons, survived until 1939.

By the mid-1930's automobiles and trucks had rendered the three separate communities on Mauna Loa unnecessary and economically disadvantageous. Two of them were demolished and all employees were concentrated in the remaining settlement near the top of the hill, the present community of Maunaloa. To accomplish this centralization, additional family dwellings were built. A few dormitories and dwellings in the Hoolehua plain for employees of the then separately managed Hoolehua fields were maintained until recent times. A program of modernization to eliminate the remaining outdoor and communal bath and toilet facilities was initiated at Maunaloa. By the early 1940's mechanization of plantation operations had reduced the number of employees, and living quarters stood vacant. Dormitories and communal messes were then razed, and unoccupied dwellings erected as family houses became the residences of single men.

In the days of separate camps there was virtually no social solidarity on a community-wide basis. Most employees regarded employment and residence in the plantation communities as temporary. When they had accumulated money, they would return to the Philippines or Japan or move on to greener pastures. Unable to speak English and often poorly skilled in Pidgin English, the Filipinos, Japanese, Chinese, and Koreans were unable—and doubtless frequently unwilling—to establish social rapport. Haoles were very few in number, and the social gulf which separated them from the ordinary workmen was so great that relations between them resembled those of lord and vassal. Filipinos were divided among themselves. Visayans, then numerically important, held aloof from the growing body of Ilocanos who soon greatly outnumbered them, and social separation if not active hostility between the two groups was marked. Personal friendships certainly existed, but there were few bonds of land, home, hearth, and kinship to tie people to the community of Maunaloa until the plantation had been in operation for about fifteen years.

Such solidarity as exists today seems to have had its first real growth at the time of the consolidation and centralization of the plantation communities in the mid-1930's, when plantation personnel had come to include a large number of employees with families. After the appearance of families, the gambling, fighting, and prostitutes of pioneer days were no longer appropriate. The plantation had become a place to bring up children under the proper atmosphere, and not a temporary work camp of womenless men with few inhibitions placed upon their conduct. Single men were thrust into the background, and the needs of families dominated all community affairs.

By the late 1930's Maunaloa had become a peaceful community, its quiet marred only occasionally by quarrels and violence over women and gambling. Most of the young employees in clerical and minor supervisory positions were now Hawaii-born nisei with high-school educations, and a generation of young people had passed through adolescence as members of the community.

In the technological sphere many and great changes had occurred. Since establishment of the plantation in 1923, mechanization has followed an irregular upward swing, broken during World War II and the early postwar period by a long plateau when little change occurred. The end of the war brought unionization, with financial demands which had to be met and spiraling costs for all commodities and services. Mechanical equipment and scientific aids of many kinds came with increasing rapidity soon after the end of World War II. By 1956 many of the techniques of 1946 or even of 1950 had become antiquated.

Improved technology has meant greatly increased specialization. New machines created jobs for operators as well as for mechanics, all at higher rates of pay. Specialization in supervisory categories also increased, but the number of field laborers and thus the total personnel was much reduced.

The gross number of employees had always varied somewhat in accordance with the yield, which in turn depended upon rainfall and, formerly, insect infestation. Other factors beyond mechanization and size of crop affected and sometimes continue to affect demands for labor. Despite lowered yields in any given year, all the customary tasks beyond harvesting must be performed and fields must be planted for harvest in subsequent years; hence large if not full crews are required. A season of very heavy rainfall might serve not only to produce a large crop but also to encourage many weeds; in former years, extraordinary labor was sometimes required for their removal.

The trend has been toward greatly increased yields produced by a much smaller number of employees. Although a serious drought halved the normal crop in 1954, the average yield per acre for the period 1951–1955 was nearly three times the annual average of that of 1926–1930 (table 10). Production in 1956, a good year from the standpoint

TABLE 10

PLANTATION PRODUCTION

Years	Index [a]
1926–1930	100
1931–1935	207
1936–1940	214
1941–1945	130 [b]
1946–1950	148 [b]
1951–1955	272 [c]
1956	335

[a] Based on average annual yields in tons of pineapple per acre under cultivation. The period 1926–1930 has been arbitrarily chosen as the base for index. A small first crop was harvested in 1925.
[b] Reflects wartime and early postwar shortages of labor and equipment as well as other factors.
[c] Production during two of these five years was seriously reduced by drought.

of rainfall, exceeded three times the average yield of 1926–1930. This threefold increase probably is considerably greater than that of other plantations of Hawaii, since it reflects a technological mastery over the handicap of inadequate rainfall, a problem which is less serious or does not exist for other plantations.

By 1956 mechanization had so reduced the requirements for field laborers that the same number of men engaged during the height of harvest in the mid-1930's could operate a modern plantation of twice the acreage. By 1956 the number employed in skilled and semiskilled positions had almost doubled, and the number of supervisory employees in relation to hourly workers had also increased. Including semiskilled workers, specialists comprised approximately 50 per cent of all personnel in December, 1956, as opposed to less than 25 per cent twenty years earlier. At the same time, the gross number of hourly employees was reduced by more than half (table 11).

TABLE 11

ANNUAL MINIMAL AND MAXIMAL NUMBERS
OF PLANTATION HOURLY EMPLOYEES

Year	Maximum (July)	Minimum (Dec.)
1936	1,289	1,109
1937	1,696	867
1938	1,409	652
1939	1,014	699
1940	793	538
1941	727	622
1942	736	568
1943	804	617
1944	828	632
1945	847	584
1946	898	619
1947	761	715
1948	840	736 [a]
1949	695	596 [b]
1950	804	748
1951	946	717
1952	940	725
1953	928	598
1954	644	511
1955	730	507
1956	709	411

[a] Acreage permanently increased by approximately 2.3 per cent.
[b] Acreage permanently increased by approximately 1 per cent.

A comparison of man-hours of labor by hourly employees since 1951 (table 12) points out sharply the effect of technological change. Man-hours of labor during 1956 were approximately half those of 1951, although annual yields in 1956 were somewhat greater.

The plantation of 1956 is an efficient, modern factory which depends upon hand labor only where it has been unable to devise machines. It represents a remarkable adjustment between the demands of modern industry, on the one hand, and, on the other hand, the force of well-established and often incompatible custom on the part of its personnel.

Changes in the social sphere reflect the interplay of these two sets of factors.

Like other small rural communities in the United States, Maunaloa has come into increasingly close contact with its neighboring communities and with the world. The illiterate or poorly educated foreign-born still constitute the majority of its residents, but the level of education has risen as the American-born children have matured and as the demand for educated specialists has grown.

TABLE 12

ANNUAL HOURS WORKED BY HOURLY EMPLOYEES

Year	Total Man-hours	Plantation production index [a]
1951	1,693,067	100.0
1952	1,408,511	96.2
1953	1,204,999	80.0 [b]
1954	927,864	50.8 [b]
1955	961,883	100.8
1956	894,719	105.1

[a] Based on 1951 tonnage.
[b] Reflects effects of serious drought.

Interest in and awareness of the outside world are indicated by the number of English newspapers which reach the community. At one time in the early 1930's only four copies of English newspapers and an undetermined but small number of copies of foreign papers, principally Japanese, were regularly received by residents of the community, but in 1956 about 160 people subscribed to Honolulu newspapers in the English language.

Other important agencies which helped to end the near-isolation of the community were radio, television, and telephones (which first became available at reasonable rates in 1951). Even more important was the construction in the early 1950's of a good hard-surfaced road connecting Maunaloa with all major communities of the island and with the airport. Children helped reduce the cultural isolation of their parents by bringing home new ideas and values learned at school.

Increased income, relative as well as absolute, has encouraged communication with the outside world and assimilation of American customs. By Hawaiian standards the plantation laborer of today is by no means impoverished, and his financial status has improved at a rate relatively faster than that of the rise in the cost of living. Before World War II, employees received only small cash wages, insufficient to allow college education for their children, extensive travel to outside communities, or the ownership of automobiles. Because of increased cash incomes together with a low cost of living, the ordinary man can afford many things which formerly were luxuries. The extension of credit to plantation workmen—a circumstance almost unthinkable before World War II—brought within reach much that had been unattainable.

The outside world thus touches the community today in many ways, and direct contact by means of car and airplane is greatly increased over former times. These developments, all unremarkable for most American communities, are noteworthy here because they represent unusually rapid change among immigrants whose culture was vastly different from that of the American-born.

The most isolated enclave is to be found among the single Filipino men, some of whom even today rarely leave the community of Maunaloa. (In 1941 one of these men stated, with evident pride, that he had been outside the community only once in fifteen years.) Lacking children to help introduce them to American ways, and hindered by illiteracy and an imperfect knowledge of English, they retain their native culture much more than others, and keep to themselves.

Following the trend among business corporations in the United States, the years have brought changing conceptions of employee welfare. Recreational facilities had received early attention in the form of athletic events for adult males. At one time the plantation is said to have sought for employment men who were skilled at boxing (a sport since abandoned) and basketball. As families came socially to dominate single men, recreational facilities for children were provided, at first almost entirely by the public school. By the mid-1930's the welfare of employees was considered a matter of importance by corporation management. A personnel manager was added to the administrative staff in 1937. Soon thereafter, the plumbing and electrical facilities of the community were improved and pension and vacation plans applying to all employees were begun. A strike of plantation workmen in 1937 doubtless stimulated these attempts at bettering conditions of work, although the strikers never clearly stated their specific grievances.

The unionization of the plantation nearly a decade later might be viewed objectively as something less than the radical, outside-motivated change that many employees consider it to be. The union demands for increased wages, fringe benefits, and theoretically impartial arbitration of employee grievances had been developing slowly for a number of years. Thus the benefits received from unionization were not out-and-out innovations. The trend was already well under way, a movement away from paternalism and toward increasing regard for the well-being of employees as a humanitarian obligation as well as a profitable economic investment.

One of the most notable changes in plantation social life has been the decrease in paternalism. Both Japanese and Filipino employees came to Hawaii with a background of experience from childhood to maturity of highly personalized social relationships. Paternalistic attitudes and practices, accompanied by a great social breach between the boss and the worker, had long existed on the sugar plantations of Hawaii and were carried over to the newer pineapple industry. The pineapple plantations thus provided an atmosphere fairly familiar to the foreign-born employees, who as small farmers and tenant-farmers in their homelands had many social and economic superiors and commonly also had patrons. For employees born in Japan, where social relationships tended to be vertically arranged, the parallel was particularly close.

In Japan, especially in rural areas and in small industries, when the ties and resources of kinship failed to meet economic or other circumstances, it was customary to make unrelated people into quasi-relatives and thus to rely upon them. The most common form of fictive kinship in Japan was a father-child relationship (*oyabun-kobun*), applying among adults, whereby the "father" served as sponsor, guarantor, guardian, friend, and frequently also lessor of land or employer. The "child" was given the opportunity to earn a livelihood while at the same time providing economic benefit for his "father." Although a great social gap might exist between fictive father and child, the relationship was highly personalized and the obligations which it entailed were regarded as moral compulsions, more binding than a legal contract.

Transplanted to Hawaii, the issei brought the custom of *oyabun-kobun* with them, applying it where it met needs, as among small merchants and the independent coffee farmers of the Kona region of the Island of Hawaii. But the circumstances of life on pineapple plantations provided no encouragement for the growth of this custom. Whether the formalized *oyabun-kobun* institution of Japan ever existed at Maunaloa is uncertain. Less formal relationships similar to the *oyabun-kobun* appear, however, to have existed in the early years of the plantation, when conditions were more conducive to their growth. And the evidence is clear that both intra-Japanese and intra-Filipino relations were once highly personalized.

Plantation *lunas*, both Japanese and Filipinos, formerly recruited their own gangs of workmen in much the same way as did foremen in the coal mines of Japan (who entered *oyabun-kobun* relations with their men). Additional encouragement to the establishment of paternal-filial ties between *luna* and workman came from the early plantation policy of paying field workmen by giving a lump sum to the *luna*, who divided the earnings among the members of his crew. These practices were soon abandoned in favor of hiring by a single delegated authority, and wages were paid on an individual basis.

A faint echo of paternalism comes in the lingering attempts to give Christmas presents to one's foreman and to plantation officials. In olden times gifts were not merely inexpensive tokens. A laborer might present goods which cost him a half-month's wages, and a calculating boss could profit greatly from such gratuities. A Haole supervisor of the pioneer days is said to have informed the local storekeeper of the gifts he desired, and arranged for the donors to pool their resources for the purchase of very expensive items. This man is reported to have left the plantation with a tremendous quantity (hundreds of barrels and packages, according to some reports) of rugs, silver, china, and other goods received from employees in this manner. An unscrupulous boss might even play the robber baron by commandeering goods and services from his employees when he wished to entertain lavishly.

The custom of giving presents was most common among the Japanese, but Chinese, Filipinos, and other non-Haole employees as well as outsiders who desired the good will of plantation administrators also followed it until growing opposition resulted in an official ban in the early 1930's. By this time the practice had been frowned upon for years by many supervisors, and the newer and younger among them refused outright to accept gifts of any kind.

A hint of paternalism might be said to survive in the deferential attitude of certain supervisors toward the manager, who surely embodies their conception of a paternal supporter, sponsor, and teacher.

The decline of paternalism is but one phase of a trend toward impersonality. Among the Japanese, the size and importance of the effective kin group have diminished. In Japan the traditional family was composed of a rather large group of lineal and collateral relatives who functioned as a unit rather than as an aggregation of individuals. As opposed to this traditional extended family of Japan, the small nuclear family (parents and children only) is the standard familial form among the Japanese of Maunaloa. In the Hawaiian setting, widely extended and active ties of kinship fill few needs and offer few advantages which cannot be more easily gained by other means, and ties with all except the closest relatives outside the nuclear family are comparatively weak.

One might reasonably ask how any form of the family except the nuclear could exist in Maunaloa in view of the fact that the Japanese are recent immigrants who came without relatives except for wives and sometimes children. At least one generation of children has matured in Hawaii, however, and the personnel of the traditional Japanese family (the eldest son and family head, his wife and children, his aged parents, and his unmarried brothers and sisters) are very often potentially available. Aged parents who live with their children are rare in the community. Most nisei regard this social arrangement as an undesirable practice which fosters discord.

In rural Japan, kin terms are often used in addressing unrelated persons, especially friends of one's parents, and even strangers may be so addressed. These are practices very rarely observed in Maunaloa.

The personalization of relationships remains strongest among Filipinos of the community, who comprise the only large foreign-born group stemming from a cultural tradition that emphasizes such a relationship. The fact that conditions of plantation life strongly discourage personalized relations may account for some of the discontent many Filipinos manifest. Warmly receptive to other peoples, they are perplexed and distressed by the social exclusion which they suffer.

Following Philippine style, terms of address used by Maunaloa Filipinos among themselves are likely to be diminutives or intimate variations of given names: for example, the syllable "ing" is added to an element of the Christian name so that Cristituta becomes "Tuting." Children and young people customarily address an unrelated mature Filipino woman by the Philippine equivalent of "aunt" and, with somewhat less frequency, call a mature man "uncle."

Ties of kinship with relatives in Hawaii tend to be close. A surprising number of Filipinos had male genetic relatives, usually cousins or uncles, already in residence in Hawaii at the time of their arrival. These men often served as sponsors, aiding their newly arrived relatives financially and in other ways. Ties of kinship among these collateral relatives tend to be preserved by Maunaloa Filipinos today. At times of crisis, financial or other aid may be requested from collateral relatives, who feel deeply obligated to respond. Leaves of absence taken by Filipino employees to attend funerals or weddings of relatives in other communities of Hawaii make an impressive annual total. During 1954, a year of unusually low yields of pineapple and consequent liberal granting of leaves, Filipinos took nearly 3,000 man-days for these stated purposes. Such leaves totaled approximately 1,500 man-days even in 1955, a year of heavy yields. Except for the death of a close relative, however, leave is seldom requested today during periods of heavy plantation work.

It is among the Filipinos that intimate relations are likely to exist between supervisor and worker, a circumstance officially frowned upon because it encourages favoritism. Filipino *lunas* must sometimes be cautioned against such behavior, and lectures in personnel management which *lunas* attend emphasize the importance of impartiality and the preservation of social distinctions between supervisor and worker.

As the only group in which many persons hold the same or similar occupational status, Filipinos are in a position favoring the growth of intimacy. Constant association at work over a period of years may serve to create strong bonds of friendship among field laborers. Men like to remain permanently in the same gang, to take their lunches in the company of many others, and to arrive at work early so that they may chat with friends.

Circumstances surrounding the retirement on pension in 1956 of three Filipino field laborers who planned to return to the Philippines are revealing in this connection. After all farewell parties had been held and all good-byes had been said, the men started for the airport with the personnel manager. While en route they encountered the field crew with whom they had worked for many years. In the words of the personnel manager, "I was taking the men to the airport when we passed their old gang in the fields close to the road. I stopped the car because they wanted to say good-bye again. It was quite a heart-rending scene.

I thought I would never get them off again and the other men back to work, so many tears flowed. And X [the *luna* in charge of the crew] finally laughed and said, 'I don't see why you're carrying on like this. You fight and yell among yourselves all year in the gang.' "

Human relations on a personalized level remain for most Filipinos desirable and are therefore a potential source of distress. A man who rises occupationally and becomes socially aloof is looked upon with disfavor by many as being snobbish.

Depersonalization of employee relationships is a point at issue in local union grievances. Union and management represent different views derived from markedly different cultural backgrounds. To officials of the plantation, who hold the Western attitude toward commercial relations, business is business and should not be personalized. The Filipino representatives of the local union manifest the opposing view—and thereby, curiously, hold attitudes quite at variance with the philosophy of labor unions. Despite the legal contract between the union and the corporation, which outlines the procedure to be followed in the settlement of grievances, local Filipino union representatives are strongly opposed to these formalities. They would much prefer a "man-to-man" talk with the manager. (This, however, would involve him directly in even the trivial issues normally settled at a lower level.) "Real men," as one Filipino union official expressed it, should speak from the heart and forget red tape; thus understanding might easily be reached.

The union representatives themselves may fail to realize the importance of personalized relations among their fellow workmen. In the summer of 1956, the complaint was made that injustice had been done because a number of unskilled seasonal employees, who are not union members, had been assigned to a category of labor paying a slightly higher rate than that of some regular employees who belonged to the union. Assignment of union members to the premium work would have required the splitting of a regular crew of workmen, and this was avoided. After a series of conferences, it was found that the regular workmen themselves valued more highly the company of their habitual associates than they did the higher wages—and the grievance dissolved.

One indication of depersonalization of relationships among Filipinos is the path which fictive kin relationships among them have taken. The Spanish-derived *compadrazgo* ("co-parenthood"), a form of godparenthood, is old in the Philippines and may have had aboriginal antecedents.

Compadrazgo in the Philippines was more than a fleeting ritual relationship associated with Catholicism. Godparent and godchild traditionally gave each other mutual support, the godparent sponsoring, advising, and giving economic aid, and the godchild, after reaching maturity, reciprocating if the godparent should fall into need. Godparent and godchild might be genetically or affinally related or might be entirely unrelated.

Following custom, one takes godparents at baptism, confirmation, and marriage, and the relationship actively continues after these events. The traditional relationship is not merely between an individual and his godparents but sets up a network of kinlike bonds. Parents and godparents become to one another *comare* and *compare* (from the Spanish *compadre* and *comadre*, "co-father" and "co-mother"), terms which Maunaloa Filipinos translate into English as "god-sister" and "godbrother." The children of *compare* and *comare* become brothers and sisters to each other, and the children of the fictive brothers and sisters become their nephews and nieces. Fictive relatives—godparents, genetic parents, and their families—are thus brought into closer relationship and might also function as a social group providing mutual aid.

In Hawaii, where other agencies have taken over many of the old functions of kinship, we might expect the *compadrazgo* to survive only in skeletal form, as a functionless ritual relationship sponsored by the Church. But at Maunaloa, and probably among the Filipino population of Hawaii as a whole, the custom seems to have grown tremendously in importance. Since the end of World War II, Ilocano parents of Maunaloa have tended to select an ever larger number of persons—as many as forty to fifty—to serve as godparents for their children. Godfathers sometimes outnumber godmothers, as there are many more Filipino men than women in the community. Although single men do not mingle much with families, a father frequently asks those with whom he works to act as godfathers.

The mushrooming of *compadrazgo* appears to be in contradiction to tendencies of social change noted elsewhere in the world. When we examine this custom, however, we find that it is so altered in structure and function that it bears little resemblance to the old *compadrazgo* of the Phillipines. Maunaloa godparents do not become advisers, sponsors, and helpers, and no favors are expected from godchildren later in life. Older men and especially older women may have so many godchildren that merely recounting their names is a feat of memory. Godparents of today are expected to give presents to the child, but this terminates their obligation. In return, they are invited to participate in a banquet which gives prestige to all concerned and especially to the genetic parents. Godchildren may still address some of their godparents by the traditional kin terms, but these forms of address have fallen out of use for ritual brothers and sisters. Among Visayans, the number of ritual parents remains small, but parties are on a grander scale and, beyond the moment, the *compadrazgo* is usually without function. The non-ritual aspects of the modern Maunaloa *compadrazgo* thus seem to have become only forms of conspicuous consumption and, for the Ilocanos, a means of providing some reimbursement for the hosts' expenditures.

The decline in official paternalism reflects in part changed cultural conditions among the employees. The immigrants and their offspring have adapted to American ways and to each other. Close supervision is unnecessary to maintain peace in the settlement and acceptable standards of sanitation and morality. Especially in regard to the welfare of their wives and children, plantation workmen have come to have vested interests in community affairs.

Unionization brought the end of paternalism in the form of rent-free housing, medical care, and the other small perquisites of former times. At the same time it introduced between boss and worker a theoretical impersonal third body, the union itself.

Another indication of the decline of paternalism is afforded by the roster of guests invited to participate in important social events in the lives of plantation workmen. In former times, plantation officials, especially the manager and his wife, were automatically invited to attend weddings, other great festivities, and funerals. Such invitations today are more likely to be made only if personal friendship—at least, fairly extensive personal contact—exists. In his capacity as guest, the boss is much less the patron than in former times.

The recent trend for employees, including supervisors, to live in homes outside the plantation community will doubtless increase the impersonality of relations among plantation personnel. Twenty years ago, employees were expected to use the housing provided for them by the company. No houses were available for rent outside the community, and workers did not earn sufficient money to purchase homes and automobiles. Today, residence in the community is not mandatory, and a small but increasing number of employees live outside, where they generally own their own homes or are purchasing them on contract.

An additional trend of change is a narrowing of the social breach between peoples of varied racial-cultural affiliation. As they have become culturally more alike, and have intermarried and produced offspring, social distances between them have diminished. Haoles and other peoples of the plantation intermix socially, on terms approaching equality, more frequently than they did twenty years ago. For the most part, however, only the Hawaii-born among the non-Haoles have appreciably narrowed the social gap which separates the Haole elite from all others.

This is not to say that old barriers imposed by differences in racial-cultural affiliation have disappeared. But interethnic attitudes of social depreciation appear always to have depended more on such considerations as relative degree of education and economic status than on an unreasoning basis of race. Whatever the ingredients of intergroup social discrimination, whatever the ratio of race prejudice as against other factors, the barriers by group have weakened. Social status increasingly accords with occupational rank on an individual basis and appears to depend less upon racial-cultural assignment.

Closely associated with the trend toward conferring social status on an individual basis is the emergence of social classes founded upon a combination of ethnic affiliation and occupational status. As yet imperfectly defined, awareness of these strata has hardly penetrated the consciousness of most persons, who see only distinct ethnic groups which they arrange in various orders of social prestige.

The growth of impersonality and individualism is an observable fact about which there can be little argument. The factors which lie behind this development, however, may have more than one interpretation. One hypothesis is that the change in the relations among foreign-born workmen is the result of the diffusion of American culture or, to put it differently, emulation of the Haole occupational and social superiors. Diffusion of Western culture is important, but to offer it as a final explanation of social changes misses much that is more fundamental. Depersonalization has applied to those emulated on the plantation as well as to their followers, and both the degree and the pattern of change have varied by racial-cultural group, depending upon cultural background and occupational rank. Moreover, the social trends we have noted are observable in all industrialized and urbanized nations of the world.

A second hypothesis, which appears more satisfactory, is that the social changes are the functional correlates of industrialization. Concomitants of industrialization have everywhere included intense specialization in labor leading to diverse interests and differentials of wealth which serve as the bases of social groupings. One of the most important correlates of industrialization has been the growth of a full reliance upon money economy. In the United States and other nations rich in natural resources, industrialization has exerted a strong influence on social organization. Among other things, it has promoted impersonality in economic relations, individualism, and a class-structured society. At the same time it has weakened the ties of kinship and made the small nuclear family the only important body of kin. Impersonal institutions and agencies, especially welfare programs and legal machinery, now take care of many needs formerly served by relatives and friends.

In Japan, a nation heavily industrialized but poorly endowed in natural resources and eking out a marginal existence, social developments have taken much the same direction as in the United States. In the period of less than a century since the beginning of the industrialization of Japan, the nuclear family has come numerically to dominate over the traditional extended family. Kinship and personal ties are stronger in modern Japan, however, because the nation, as well as being less highly industrialized than the United States, has lacked the economic surplus to develop fully the agencies which have served functionally as the economic surrogates of kinship in the United States.

Coming from peasant societies where kinship and kinlike bonds were strong, the Japanese and Filipinos of Maunaloa did not immediately or entirely relinquish the practices of paternalism and personalization of relationships to which they had been accustomed from birth. Filipinos attempted to follow the old patterns with everyone. Japanese held chiefly to themselves and, in a filial mold, to those in authority above them.

In the early days the plantation, in the persons of its officials, was the powerful patron who provided employment and protection, and watched over the workmen to ensure that they followed the rules of the new land. The recruiting of men by their future foreman and the collective payment of workmen through the foreman were hardly impersonal. The relatively few occupational distinctions among the foreign-born employees, the isolation of the community, and the scarcity of money also fostered personalization.

Plantation economy had included what might be called payment in kind, the perquisites of former days. Employees then ordinarily received little hard cash. Despite its relative scarcity, however, money had always served the immigrant laborers in the new land as the most important substitute for kinlike relations. In more accurate terms, money partially displaced rather than substituted for kinship. As time passed, the foreign-born gradually relinquished their old patterns of behavior and adjusted to the new. The new patterns increasingly emphasized the role of money, making it available in greater amounts, and making personalization progressively inappropriate and difficult.

New technology meant increased efficiency achieved in part through increased specialization. Machine technology created a wider range of distinction in employee skills and wages than had formerly existed. Earnings depended upon individual knowledge, talent, and performance. Money, the most impersonal of yardsticks, had become ever more the measure of individual worth and the means of meeting needs. Money also encouraged the growth of social distinctions based upon one's capacity to earn it.

With the development of many levels of skill, authority, and compensation at work, the Japanese have come to constitute a class markedly elevated above the Filipinos. At the same time the rating of the individual on the basis of his own qualifications for plantation work has weakened the social barriers between ethnic groups.

Many of the social changes which we have noted thus appear to be the unplanned consequences of industrialization. Even among the groups and individuals most strongly encapsulated in foreign culture, the demands of industry have exercised a strong influence.

IX | *Summary and Conclusions*

The Hawaiian plantation town of Maunaloa does not meet the stereotype of a rural community. Contrary to popular conception, life is not rural in the sense that relationships are personalized and egalitarian, or—as in some areas of the world where Western industry has placed foreign masters over serflike natives employed in agricultural industry —personalized and paternalistic. Life is not rural in the old-fashioned sense of near self-sufficiency. Subsistence is gained from cash wages earned from a single crop, and wage work represents the only economically important effort. The very few persons who substantially add to their wages do so by engaging in part-time enterprises, such as the gas station, which provide necessary services. Home industry is on so small a scale that its contribution to domestic economy is negligible. Virtually the only other attempt to augment income is through gambling among Filipinos, a practice which has motives beyond the desire for commercial gain.

A veneer of the rural comes from the setting of the community, the atmosphere of informality which characterizes all of Hawaii, and the fact that most of the employees were reared as peasants. Relationships among these employees and other residents of Maunaloa, however, are not those of a peasant farming community, but more nearly approximate those of an urban industrial plant. The plantation is, in fact, most aptly described as a farm factory or "factory in the field." [1] an industrial concern whose product is agricultural.

In its operation as a factory, the plantation imposes demands which have had a culturally leveling influence upon its employees. Filipinos, Japanese, and other plantation peoples come from cultural backgrounds in which values and personal relationships are very different from those of the efficient, modern factory. To remold the attitudes of these men

[1] From Carey McWilliams, *Factories in the Field* (Boston, Little, Brown and Co., 1939).

into patterns compatible with factory organization has been a process of continued adaptation. It has required not only time but also the elimination of the unmalleable.

Foreign-born employees have retained in full force only those elements of their native cultures which are neutral so far as effective operation of the plantation is concerned. Whether a worker subsists on a Filipino diet or an American diet, for example, is of no consequence to the company, provided he is in good health. Regular attendance at work and conformance with many other American social norms, however, are matters of importance.

The more noteworthy characteristics of modern Maunaloa life are tabulated below. By way of caution, however, it must be added that many of the following statements represent trends rather than complete developments.

1. Absolute reliance on money economy, based upon the intensive and highly mechanized cultivation of a single crop.
2. Depersonalization of relationships of employees and increased importance of the individual, fostered by reliance upon money and the concomitant growth of pension plans, unionization, and credit unions.
3. Decreased importance of kinship and fictive kinship, and emergence of the nuclear family as the only familial form.
4. Emergence of social classes based upon a combination of occupational status and ethnic affiliation.
5. Increased emphasis on social status according to occupation, which weakens personal ties and obscures hierarchical social distinctions by ethnic affiliation.
6. Social separation of ethnic groups decreasing as they become culturally more alike.
7. Socioeconomic mobility limited by ethnic affiliation but increased over former times.
8. Cultural conformity among all peoples to demands imposed by the nature of plantation life, and retention of only that foreign culture which is not actively inimical to efficient industry. Foreign-born single men least well adjusted to American culture.
9. Highly secularized life, with a sharp decline in foreign practices of supernaturalism.

10. Increased awareness of and contact with the external world.
11. Community solidarity inhibited by the presence of several ethnic groups and a disproportionate number of single men, but increasing as intergroup social and cultural distinctions diminish.

To what extent do the foregoing statements apply to corporation-owned plantation communities in other areas of the world? The data that have been published indicate conformity in general but divergence in detail.[2] The community of Maunaloa is probably more complex socially than most of its foreign counterparts because of the unusually large number of racial-cultural strains among its personnel and the long-established attitudes concerning the relative superiority and inferiority of these groups. At the same time, a somewhat contrary but also long-established Hawaiian tradition opposes sharp inequalities on a "racial" basis. Social changes which have occurred at Maunaloa appear to constitute greater development of trends noticeable in foreign plantations, which are less highly mechanized and do not offer their personnel such favorable economic conditions.

To what extent is Maunaloa typical of the Hawaiian pineapple industry? For lack of adequate factual data, the answer must depend in part upon impressions. In technological matters Maunaloa plantation is among the more advanced but is not markedly differentiated from others. In the composition of its personnel it differs chiefly in having a larger number of single men. Trends of change in technology and community life have been closely similar everywhere. It is interesting to note that the plantation commonly regarded by men in the pineapple industry as the most "old-fashioned" in all respects except technology has followed, in its principal aspects, the pattern of social change noted for Maunaloa. Although it is the lone pineapple plantation whose workmen are not unionized, an employee council operates for collective, impersonal negotiation with management, and forms what may be described as an independent company union which uses the activities of the official union as a guide.

The fact that Maunaloa is operated by a mainland concern and staffed by supervisory employees from the mainland gives it a flavor

---

[2] See, for example, Julian Steward *et al.*, *The People of Puerto Rico* (University of Illinois Press, 1956), and H. W. Hutchinson, *Village and Plantation Life in Northeastern Brazil* (The University of Washington Press, 1957).

distinctive from that of Hawaiian-owned plantations. Relationships among plantation personnel of Maunaloa seem somewhat less personalized and paternalistic than those of Hawaiian concerns. Other differences might stem from the fact that Maunaloa is one of the plantations most isolated from the city of Honolulu. But the sum of all differences is small, and the observations which have been made about Maunaloa seems to fit other Hawaiian plantations and plantation communities with little major alteration.

The future of Hawaiian plantation communities seems fairly clear. Plantation towns were founded and operated out of necessity to meet circumstances that are ceasing to exist. Employees have become sufficiently Americanized in attitudes and moral standards; protective custody and surveillance of their private lives is no longer necessary. When housing and other purchasable necessities are available through private enterprise, the principal reason for these communities will cease to exist. Initial steps in this direction have already been taken. Company-operated stores are now less common, and the Maunaloa trend toward living outside the plantation community applies to other plantations also. In 1956 one of the largest plantations offered the dwellings of its community for sale to employees. Plantation communities in the sense of communities composed mainly of employees may continue to exist in the less well settled areas of Hawaii. As corporation-owned settlements, however, such communities appear doomed to extinction. It seems safe to prophesy that plantation management will view their disappearance with few regrets as relief from a burden peripheral to their principal interests and outside their sphere of special competence.

When the plantation town disappears, plantations will indeed be factories and the relationships among their personnel will be little distinguished from those of any industrial concern.

Index